Same Team – A Street Soccer Story

Robbie Gordon and Jack Nurse

methuen | drama

LONDON • NEW YORK • OXFORD • NEW DELHI • SYDNEY

METHUEN DRAMA
Bloomsbury Publishing Plc
50 Bedford Square, London, WC1B 3DP, UK
1385 Broadway, New York, NY 10018, USA
29 Earlsfort Terrace, Dublin 2, Ireland

BLOOMSBURY, METHUEN DRAMA and the Methuen
Drama logo are trademarks of Bloomsbury Publishing Plc

First published in Great Britain 2023

Cover image: Tommy Ga-Ken Wan

Cover design: Serden Salih

A catalogue record for this book is available from the British Library.

Library of Congress Control Number: 2023948900

ISBN: PB: 978-1-3504-5934-2
ePDF: 978-1-3504-5935-9
eBook: 978-1-3504-5936-6

Series: Modern Plays

Typeset by Mark Heslington Ltd, Scarborough, North Yorkshire

Same Team
A Street Soccer Story

**By Robbie Gordon & Jack Nurse,
story created with the women
of Dundee Change Centre**

Cast

Chloe-Ann Tylor	JO
Hannah Jarrett-Scott	THE B
Hiftu Quasem	NOOR
Louise Ludgate	LORRAINE
Neshla Caplan	SAMMY

Creative Team

Robbie Gordon & Jack Nurse	Writers
Bryony Shanahan	Director
Alisa Kalyanova	Set & Costume Designer
Lizzie Powell	Lighting Designer
Susan Bear	Sound Designer
Zephyr Liddell	Costume Supervisor

Production Team

Kevin McCallum	Head of Production
Renny Robertson	Head of Lighting & Sound
Dave Bailey	Lighting & Sound Technician
Fi Elliott	Lighting & Sound Technician
Yvonne Buskie	Company Stage Manager
Kara Jackson	Deputy Stage Manager
Chris Mundy	Assistant Stage Manager

The Street Soccer Players

Borghild Townsley
Kirsty Oliphant
Jennie Thomson
Eilidh Anderson
Zara Knight
Jennifer Garty
Candice Lawrence
Sarah Henderson

Robbie Gordon is a theatre-maker and creative engagement specialist based in Scotland.

He is the Creative Engagement Director at the Traverse Theatre and joint Artistic Director of Wonder Fools alongside Jack Nurse.

He is the co-creator of *Positive Stories for Negative Times*, an international participatory project reaching over 9,000 young people in seventeen countries culminating in four regional festivals at the Gaiety Theatre, Traverse Theatre, Eden Court and Perth Theatre.

As a writer: *549: Scots of the Spanish Civil War*, *The Coolidge Effect*, *McNeill of Tranent*, *Ozymandias* (Wonder Fools), *When the Sun Meets the Sky* (Traverse Theatre/Capital Theatres).

Selected other work: Director and producer of *Class Act* (Traverse Theatre); Director of *Ayr Gaiety's Culture Collective* projects with Jack Nurse; Co-creator of the New Scottish Companies Programme (Ayr Gaiety); lead artist (Ayrshire) on Danny Boyle's *Pages of the Sea* (National Theatre of Scotland and 1418 NOW); Co-Movement Director of *The Enemy* (National Theatre of Scotland); Movement Director of *Svengali* (Eve Nicol and Pitlochry Festival Theatre); Associate Director of *Square Go* (Francesca Moody Productions).

Jack Nurse is a director and theatre-maker. He co-founded Glasgow-based theatre company Wonder Fools in 2014. Jack is an Artist in Residence (Creative Development) at the Traverse Theatre and co-artistic lead of the international participatory project *Positive Stories for Negative Times*.

Training: Royal Conservatoire of Scotland and the National Theatre Studio Directors' Course.

As Director/Writer: *549: Scots of the Spanish Civil War*, *The Coolidge Effect* (Wonder Fools); *When the Sun Meets the Sky* (Traverse Theatre/Capital Theatres).

As Director: *24 (Day): The Measure of My Dreams* and *The Essence of the Job Is Speed* (Almeida Theatre); *And Then Come the Nightjars* (Wonder Fools); *Lampedusa* (Citizens Theatre/Wonder Fools); *Meet Jan Black* (Wonder Fools/Ayr Gaiety); *Larchview* (National Theatre of Scotland/BBC Scotland); *The Lost Elves* (Citizens Theatre/RCS); *The Mack*, *The Storm* (A Play, A Pie and A Pint/Traverse Theatre).

As Associate/Assistant Director, Jack has worked with National Theatre of Scotland, HOME, Sell A Door, Citizens Theatre, Music & Lyrics, and the Royal Lyceum Theatre Edinburgh.

Bryony Shanahan is a freelance Theatre Director. Between 2019 and 2023 she was Joint Artistic Director of the Royal Exchange Theatre, Manchester. She was the recipient of the Genesis Future Directors Award. Theatre work includes:

For the Royal Exchange: *Bloody Elle* (West End, Traverse Theatre, Soho Theatre, Royal Exchange); *No Pay? No Way!*; *Beginning*; *Let The Right One In*; *Nora: A Doll's House*; *Wuthering Heights*; *Queens of the Coal Age*; *Weald*; and *Nothing*.

Other theatre credits include: *Trade* (Young Vic); *Enough* (Traverse); *Chicken Soup* (Sheffield Theatres), *Operation Crucible* (59E59 NYC, Sheffield Crucible, national tour); *Bitch Boxer* (Soho Theatre, national tour); *Boys Will Be Boys* (National Theatre); *Chapel Street* (national tour); *You and Me* (Greenwich Theatre & national tour).

Alisa Kalyanova is a Designer based in Glasgow. She studied Visual Communication and Graphic Design at the Iceland University of the Arts in Reykjavik before training in Set and Costume Design at the Royal Conservatoire of Scotland in Glasgow.

Recent theatre credits include: *Fedora, Alice's Adventures in Wonderland* (IF Opera); *Love the Sinner* (Vanishing Point); *Exodus, The Strange Case of Dr Jekyll & Mr Hyde* (National Theatre of Scotland); *The Bacchae, Julius Caesar* (Company of Wolves); *Wolfie, hang, The Mistress Contract* (Tron Theatre); *The Summoning of Everyman, Taming of the Shrew* (Royal Conservatoire of Scotland); *The Last Forecast, Kissing Linford Christie* (Catherine Wheels); *Chaos* (Perth Theatre); *Cinderella, Sleeping Beauty, Jamie and the Unicorn* (Ayr Gaiety Theatre – costumes only); *Figaro, The Merry Widow* (Opera Bohemia); *Robin Hood* (Cumbernauld Theatre).

Lizzie Powell is a Lighting Designer whose theatre work includes: *August Osage County* (Malmo Stadsteater); *The Grand Old Opera House Hotel* (Traverse Theatre); *What Girls are Made Of* (Traverse Theatre/Raw Material Arts); *Cat on a Hot Tin Roof, The Mountaintop, Mother Courage, Anna Karenina, The Mighty Walzer* (Royal Exchange, Manchester); *Macbeth – An Undoing* (Royal Lyceum Edinburgh); *The*

Young/Tron Theatre); *Shark in the Park* (Macrobert Arts Centre/ Assembly Rooms); *The Choir* (Citizens Theatre/ATG); and *Beauty and the Beast* (Glasgow Life).

Her film, radio, and voiceover credits include: *Rebus* (Eleventh Hour Films); *The Rig* S1 & S2 (Amazon Prime Video); *Scot Squad* (BBC Comedy Unit); *Adam* (BBC/National Theatre of Scotland/Hopscotch Films); *Christmas Tales* (Royal Lyceum Edinburgh); *Too Rough* (BFI); *Scenes For Survival – Future Perfect Tense* (National Theatre of Scotland); *This Thing of Darkness* S2, *From Fact to Fiction: After Midnight* (BBC Radio); and *The Bard's Tale* (inXile Entertainment).

She recently completed another feature film, *Sebastian* (BFI/Creative Scotland). She is due to star in *The Rig* S2 (Amazon Prime Video).

Hiftu also appears in *The Witcher: Blood Origin* and *The Witcher* S3 (Netflix); *Granite Harbour* (BBC Scotland); *Killing Eve, This Is Going to Hurt, Trigonometry, The Nest* and *Traces* (BBC); and *Endeavour* (ITV).

Hiftu began her career acting in a range of short films such as *Tehzeeb* and *Meet Me By the Water*. Her theatre credits include *Miss Julie* (Perth Theatre at Horsecross Arts/Scottish Tour); *Fission* (Seven Dials Playhouse); and *At Home I Speak* (Rich Mix Theatre).

Louise Ludgate was born in Aberdeen and trained at the Royal Conservatoire of Scotland. She has worked with a multitude of theatre companies including the Traverse Theatre, the Tron Theatre, the Sherman Theatre, National Theatre, Headlong, Birmingham Rep, The Citizens Theatre, Stellar Quines, Lung Ha Theatre Company, A Play A Pie and A Pint, The Arches, Magnetic North, Paines Plough, The Royal Court, Dundee Rep, National Theatre of Scotland, Vanishing Point, Fire Exit, Manchester Royal Exchange, Ten Feet Tall, Actors Touring Company, Suspect Culture, the Bush, Lookout and the King's Theatre.

Television and film credits include: *Mayflies, Spooks, River City, Glasgow Kiss, Romance Class, Freedom, The Key* and *Sea of Souls* (BBC); *Payback, Taggart* and *High Times* (ITV).

Short film credits include: *Nature Nurture* (Molloy); *Floating Worlds* (Eatough); *Swung* (Sigma); *The Elemental* (Northlight); and *Nightpeople* (Newfoundland). Radio credits include: *The Breach, For the Love of Leo, Wax Fruit, Personal Best* and many others.

Neshla Caplan trained at the Royal Conservatoire of Scotland in Musical Theatre.

Her theatre credits include: *An Oak Tree, Arabian Nights, The BFG* (Royal Lyceum Edinburgh); *Common Is As Common Does, A Memoir* (21 Common); *The Stamping Ground* (Raw Material Arts/Eden Court); *Cinderella* (Perth Theatre); *Move – Gluasad* (Disaster Plan); *The Alchemist* (Tron Theatre); *Arctic Oil, The Breakfast Plays* (Traverse Theatre); *Sunshine on Leith* (Leeds Playhouse/UK Tour); *Adam* (National Theatre of Scotland); *Celestial Body, Toy Plastic Chicken, Wee Free: The Musical, Voices In Her Ear* (A Play, A Pie and A Pint); *The Sunshine Ghost* (Festival Theatre); *Secret Show 1* (Blood Of The

Comedy of Errors, *Endgame*, *The Libertine* (Citizens Theatre); *James IV* (Raw Material Arts); *Falstaff* (Scottish Opera/Santa Fe Opera); *A Midsummer Night's Dream* (Scottish Opera); *King John*, *Macbeth* (RSC); *Avalanche: A Love Story* (Barbican/Sydney Theatre Company); *The Da Vinci Code*, *Dial M for Murder* (Simon Friend Productions); *Our Ladies of Perpetual Succour* (West End/National Theatre of Scotland); *Thrown*, *Orphans*, *Red Dust Road*, *Adam*, *Knives in Hens*, *Venus as a Boy* (National Theatre of Scotland); *Victory Condition*, *B*, *Human Animals*, *Violence and Son* (Royal Court Theatre); *Our Town* (Regent's Park Open Air Theatre); *Romeo & Juliet* (Crucible Theatre, Sheffield); *Cyrano de Bergerac* (Citizens Theatre/National Theatre of Scotland/ Royal Lyceum Edinburgh).

Susan Bear is a Sound Designer, Musician and Producer. She has worked with artists including *The Pastels Tuff Love, Pictish Trail, Martha Ffion, Malcolm Middleton* and *Karine Polwart* as a producer, songwriter, mix engineer, session musician or combination of the above.

Recent sound design/compositional work includes: theatre shows *Ode to Joy* (Stories Untold Productions); *WILF* (Traverse Theatre); a new collaboration with writer Imogen Stirling for Push the Boat Out Festival/National Theatre of Scotland; and music for short film *Air We Breathe*, in collaboration with composer Kim Moore. Her music has been used in various commercial campaigns for brands such as Volvo, ScotGov NHS, Glendronach Whisky and Caorunn Gin.

Susan also releases music under her own name – her previous two albums, *Creature* and *Alter*, received support from BBC Radio 6 Music and BBC Radio Scotland, and Spotify and Apple Music editorial playlist placement. She writes, performs, produces, records and mixes her music solo from her studio in Glasgow.

Zephyr Liddell is an Artist and Costume Designer based in Glasgow, named on Saltire Society's inaugural *40 Under 40* List in 2023.

Recent works include: *Disciples* (Stellar Quines/Traverse Theatre); *Plinth* (Al Seed/Vanishing Point); and *Forged* (Laura Fisher/Unlimited). She has designed for numerous companies including Scottish Dance Theatre, Mele Broomes, Farah Saleh and Bassline Circus. Zephyr works as a Costume Supervisor, most recently on: *A Mother's Song* (Macrobert Arts Centre/KT Producing); *Walking with the Ancestors in Joy and Healing* (Ashanti Harris/Tramway).

Chloe-Ann Tylor trained at the Royal Conservatoire of Scotland and graduated in 2016. She was the Citizens Theatre intern that same year, and, in 2022, was the recipient of the Philippa Bragança award for her performance in *Svengali*.

Theatre credits includes: *Battery Park* (Sleeping Warrior); *Thrown* (National Theatre of Scotland/Edinburgh International Festival); *Svengali* (Pitlochry Festival Theatre/Pleasance); *I am Tiger* (Perth Theatre/Edinburgh Children's Festival); *Doppler* (Grid Iron); *Mrs Puntila and Her Man Matti* (Royal Lyceum Edinburgh); *The Stornoway Way* (Dogstar Theatre); *Close Quarters* (Out of Joint/Sheffield Theatres); *Hansel & Gretel, Trainspotting* (Citizens Theatre); *Circle of Fifths, The Strange Case of Jekyll and Hyde* (Royal Conservatoire of Scotland); *The Merchant of Venice* (Bard in the Botanics); and *Titus Andronicus* (Dundee Rep).

Hannah Jarrett-Scott trained at the Royal Central School of Speech and Drama.

Theatre credits include: *Gunter* (Dirty Hare – Fringe First winner); *Underwood Lane* (Tron Theatre); *Alright Sunshine* (Òran Mór); *Pride and Prejudice* (*Sort of)* (Criterion Theatre, West End, UK tour & Tron Theatre – Olivier Award winner); *Cinderfella* (Tron Theatre); *The Taming of the Shrew* (Tron Theatre/Sherman Theatre); *The Wolves* (Theatre Royal Stratford East); *A Bottle of Wine and Patsy Cline* (Gilded Balloon); *A Stone's Throw* (Giddy Aunt); *Glory on Earth, The Lion, the Witch and the Wardrobe* (Royal Lyceum Edinburgh); *Once This Is All Over We Still Have To Clear Up* (Yellow Magpies); *Janis Joplin: Full Tilt* (Theatre Royal Stratford East); and *Midsummer Songs* (New Wolsey Theatre).

Television credits include: *Outlander* (Sony/Starz/LeftBank); *Two Doors Down* (BBC Studios); *Float – Series 1 & 2* (Black Camel Productions for BBC); *Annika* (Black Camel Productions for Alibi); *Scot Squad* (BBC Scotland); *Trust Me* (Red Productions for BBC); and *Short Stuff* (BBC Scotland).

Radio/Audio credits include: *Hotline* (Tron Theatre); and *Rebus* (BBC).

Hiftu Quasem is best known for her role as Misha in *Ten Percent* (Amazon Prime Video). She has completed filming *Something in the Water* (Studio Canal), a feature film directed by Hayley Easton-Street.

TRAVERSE THEATRE

Here we are – together – marking 60 years of the Traverse. Together, we celebrate six decades of stories that connect, inspire, challenge, entertain and that contribute to the cultural voice of our nation. With an abundance of shows from talented artists with urgent stories that bring life and vitality to our stages – both in-person and digital – the Traverse continues to be a platform for debate, a space for our community, and home of memorable experiences. Across our programme, you can encounter trailblazing creativity that offers unique opportunities to explore the world around us, connect with the lives of others and that spark that vital curiosity in what it is to be human.

The Traverse is a champion of performance, experience and discovery. Enabling people to access and engage with theatre is our fundamental mission, and we want our work to represent, speak to and be seen by the broadest cross section of society. We are specialists in revealing untold perspectives in innovative ways. This is our role as Scotland's premier new work theatre and a commitment that drives each strand of our work.

Our year-round programme bursts with new stories, live and digital performances that challenge, inform and entertain our audiences. We empower artists and audiences to make sense of the world today, providing a safe space to question, learn, empathise and – crucially – encounter different people and experiences. Conversation and the coming together of groups are central to a democratic society, and we champion equal expression and understanding for the future of a healthy national and international community.

The Traverse produces nationally and internationally significant work of the highest quality, with our strategic aims centred around Art, Community, Audience and Culture. We aspire to be an asset to Scottish society, support creativity, grow our impact through effective partnerships and platform a programme diverse in its form and stories. Collaborating with community and sector partners, we commission and create new work that enriches and transforms lives and is representative of all our communities.

We continue to evolve and innovate as we pass our 60th year. Our new programming model holds space in winter seasons to include community-inspired and co-produced collaborations where social issues and impact are prioritised. As Scotland's premier new work theatre, we are well positioned to augment and platform these narratives, and partner with organisations to highlight barriers and bridges experienced by our communities; from environmental phenomena which impact industries and communities to mental health and wellbeing in health sectors. By reflecting on – and connecting with – our core aims and ambitions, we recognise a present opportunity to redefine and broaden routes into artistic creation and expression. Ensuring that the work of the Traverse is sustainable and has resonance, relevance, and impact beyond already engaged groups, reaching those who may not traditionally visit the theatre or connect with the arts.

In partnership with key players from across the sector and beyond, our collaborations challenge stigma and address the needs of our communities, widening access to the arts, and highlighting the barriers experienced every day by those who are underrepresented. The Traverse partnered with Street Soccer Scotland, a charity using football for positive social change, and through the process, the players gained new tools for self-actualisation and means to engage with culture. As we platform the intertwined lived and creative experiences of Street Soccer Scotland's community, we also provide the organisation continued benefit via royalties. This model centres social impact at its core as well as enriches our partners' and own communities. This is about more than entertainment – this is about goodwill, trust and social upliftment.

Here's to the Traverse and all who have created with, played for, visited, and continue to champion everything we are. Our past successes drive our present and future direction, in the knowledge that our unique ability to nurture new talent and engage audiences through ambitious storytelling has never been more crucial in creating and sustaining a vibrant theatre landscape that reflects and challenges the world today.

Find out more about our work: traverse.co.uk

WRITERS' NOTE

As writers, we always work with communities during our process whether that be a geographical one or a group bound together by shared experience. In the past, we've worked with entire towns, the dementia friendly community and even the relatives of the Scottish members of the International Brigades. It's safe to say though that embarking on this journey with Street Soccer has probably been one of the most special of our lives.

It all started when the Traverse commissioned us, and we met David Duke (Street Soccer's Founder and CEO) to talk about the work Street Soccer do. We talked for ages about the players, their stories and the Homeless World Cup. We felt immediately inspired to pull our boots on and start working with the players.

Then the pandemic happened, and the project was put on ice for a while. But when we returned both the Traverse and Street Soccer were going through a post-lockdown recovery with many of the issues explored in the play exacerbated throughout this time.

We met Andy Hook and Sarah Rhind from Street Soccer to chat about the prospect of working with the women's team in Dundee. This was one of the hardest interviews of our lives and when we knew we were working with the right organisation. Players' welfare and experience was at the forefront of the conversation. We were galvanised by this players-first approach and how embedded it is across the organisation.

Then we visited the group for the first time and talked about what they would like to explore in the workshops, designing the future activity together. We landed on working with the players on their own writing before beginning to create the characters and story that you're about to read.

What followed, over the next year, were some of the most joyous times in our careers. We laughed, we trained, we wrote, we played games and at one point the team even made an obstacle course for us. This process culminated in a reading of the play back up at the Change Centre. Straight after, we got to watch the Street Soccer team play football with the actors and we felt the sense of community that we'd always wanted to build around the play.

This play would not have been possible without David D, David Mac, Louise, Heather, Sarah, Andy, Ross, Kyle, Scott, Ryan, Morag, Jack, all the staff at the Change Centre, Burness Paull, and the players of Street Soccer. We've always said it takes a village to make one of our plays. This one is no exception. SAME TEAM.

STREET SOCCER SCOTLAND

Street Soccer Scotland is a charity using football for positive social change. We tackle a range of social issues in a holistic way through empowerment, connection, and support. We work with people experiencing poverty, homelessness, drug and alcohol problem use, criminal justice involvement, exclusion, mental health, those in the care system and those with additional support needs.

Our mission is to create hope and opportunity for all. Our aim is to ensure everyone feels they belong, has networks of support, and can grow their confidence and skills. We want every person to feel happy and hopeful for the future.

We run football programmes across Scotland, supporting over 2,500 people of all ages and backgrounds, in 10 different local authorities.

A key element of our front line delivery is our Street 45 Programme, a Women's Programme designed and run by and for women. Street45 focuses on movement and social connection, building mental, physical and social wellbeing through 45 minutes of physical activity and 45 minutes of personal development.

94% of our players feel their life has improved since joining Street Soccer, with players making progress along their journey to their positive destinations in employment, improved mental health and more positive family relationships.

This fantastic opportunity to partner with Traverse supported by our long-term supporters at Burness Paull LLP brings a unique chance for us to unite in our mission to address the growing needs of society. Working together to challenge stigma and address the needs of our communities, bringing the arts to new audiences to highlight the challenges faced by our players every day. The players involved in the #SAMETEAM project have found new ways to express themselves and confidently share their own personal experiences bringing a new voice. Our thanks to Robbie and Jack and the whole team involved, we embrace this opportunity to work collaboratively and look forward to capturing the impact this play will have.

Burness Paull

Proudly based in Scotland, Burness Paull is a full-service, independent law firm working with leading organisations across the UK and internationally. Burness Paull is the exclusive UK member of Lex Mundi, the world's leading network of independent law firms.

As a truly independent law firm operating in a fast-moving and challenging global landscape, we have complete licence to shape our culture and determine our values in a way that sustainably supports the needs of our people, our clients, our wider community and the environment.

Connecting with our people, clients and wider communities is intrinsic to who we are. We want to form human and high-performing partnerships that make a difference.

That's why we are so pleased to have teamed up with our longstanding partners Street Soccer Scotland and the Traverse Theatre to bring to the stage *Same Team – A Street Soccer Story*, written in collaboration with the women players of Street Soccer's Change Centre.

Our partnership with Street Soccer Scotland is supported by the Burness Paull Foundation, and goes back over 10 years. We're always looking for fresh new ways to work together and to be able to collaborate with the Traverse and Street Soccer on this unique project bringing together sport, the arts and business for social change is a true demonstration of the power of innovative partnerships.

We hope everyone enjoys the play – we can't wait to see where it goes next!

With thanks

The Traverse extends grateful thanks to all of its supporters, including those who prefer to remain anonymous. Their valuable contributions ensure that the Traverse continues to champion stories and storytellers in all of its forms, help develop the next generation of creative talent and lead vital projects in our local community, Scotland and beyond.

With your help, we can write the next scene of our story.

Visit traverse.co.uk/support-us to find out more.

Individual Supporters

In Residence Partners

This Theatre has the support of the Peggy Ramsay Foundation / Film
4 Playwrights Awards Scheme.

The Traverse Theatre is further supported by **IASH**, the Institute of
Advanced Research in the Humanities, the University of Edinburgh.

Same Team – A Street Soccer Story

PRE-SHOW

We are in a space.

It could be a stage, a community hall, or even an indoor football centre.

The most important thing about this space is that the normal rules of theatre don't apply and there's enough room for a kickabout.

In this space the audience becomes the fans, clearance becomes kick-off, the interval becomes half-time.

When the fans enter, they see trials taking place on the pitch. Some are even invited to join in.

Our five characters are right in amongst it, along with real players from Street Soccer and some of the audience. They are undertaking a series of physical drills. All competing for their place in the Scotland Homeless World Cup squad.

Someone is downstage with a big drum teaching the audience chants. **The B**. *Hyping up the fans. These chants will come in useful later.*

The trials are coming to an end.

The whistle goes.

It's time to go.

Welcome to Same Team – The Street Soccer Musical: On Ice.

Only joking.

Everyone lines up waiting.

Who is going to make the cut?

SQUAD SELECTION

Jo (*to audience*) Awright? I'm Jo. Welcome to the story of my team.

The B Oi!

Jo   Oor team. The Scotland Team for the Homeless World Cup.

So we're at the trials, right? But I already ken I'm gonna get picked because I'm the best here. And then Coach goes:

Jo (*as* **Coach**)   First up – Jo. You've been Captain for the last three years but I want you to know this place is on merit.

Jo (*to audience*)   Told ye's.

Jo (*as* **Coach**)   Next on the teamsheet is – Noor. Well done this evening wee one. It's been good to meet you. You've got some skills I'll say.

Noor   Thank you so much. I'm – I'm buzzing.

Jo (*as* **Coach**)   The real work starts now though, eh?

Noor   Aye, of course.

Jo (*as* **Coach**)   Next up – Bethany, also known as The B.

The B   No Scotland, no party!

Jo (*as* **Coach**)   Thank you, B.

The B   Float like a butterfly sting like a bee, the hands can't hit what the eyes can't see. C'MON. Did you miss me Coach?

Jo (*as* **Coach**)   I'm going to miss the peace and quiet now you're back.

The B   I'll take that as a compliment.

Jo (*as* **Coach**)   Fourth in the squad – Lucinda?

Lorraine   Lorraine?

Jo (*as* **Coach**)   Lorraine! Aye sorry, Lorraine. Still getting used to some of these new faces.

Lorraine   Absolutely not a problem. I'm delighted to be selected, thank you.

Noor   Me too, Lucinda.

Lorraine Lorraine.

Noor Lorraine. Sorry. Aye.

Jo (*as* **Coach**) And finally, last place goes to . . . Sammy.

Sammy Me?

Jo (*as* **Coach**) That's your name int it?

Sammy Aye but . . . are you sure?

Jo (*as* **Coach**) Of course I'm sure. Cheers so much to everyone else, see you back at the Change Centre soon for some general sessions. Thanks again.

The players from Street Soccer and the audience exit. They look hard done by.

Jo (*as* **Coach**) Ladies. Congratulations on making the squad for the Homeless World Cup. We only have three weeks to get yous ready for Milan.

Some of you might be wondering . . . why am I here?

I remember feeling the same thing before I went to Mexico in 2012. I wondered why I'd been chosen. Why me? But this experience was the first step I took in really beginning to value myself. Which is an ongoing process, I guess . . .

The **Coach** *stares into space.*

The B Everything alright Coach?

Jo (*as* **Coach**) Oh aye, B. Home stuff. But I'm leaving that off the pitch. Before we go any further, there are six core values I need you to sign up to. Six ways that will bring us closer as a team and allow us to play to our best. Number one. Players always come first.

Nobody answers . . .

Jo (*as* **Coach**) A simple 'aye' will do. Players always come first.

All Aye.

Jo (*as* **Coach**) We look to the future.

All Aye.

Jo (*as* **Coach**) We never leave anyone behind.

All Aye.

Jo (*as* **Coach**) We place others before self.

All Aye.

Jo (*as* **Coach**) We keep our promises.

All Aye.

Jo (*as* **Coach**) And we are a family.

All Aye.

Jo (*as* **Coach**) Let me hear you?

All AYE.

Jo (*as* **Coach**) Now let's get to work.

TRAINING SESSION 1

Sammy 6am. Up.
Didn't sleep, I think.
Get out of bed.
Wee.
Shower.
Cold water.
Running through my hair.
Onto my skull.
Over my face.
Catch my breath.
Catch my breath.
Out.
Towel.
Dry.
Get dressed.

Turn the hot water on for the boys.
Dash downstairs.
Letter on the doormat.
Red writing.
Big capitals.
Not now.
4 slices of brown bread.
Butter.
Cheese on one.
Ham and cheese on the other.
Paul doesnae take ham.
8 wee triangles now.
Got to get them up.
Daryll, up.
Iron shirts.
Daryll.
Trousers.
Daryll, up.
Doomph.
He's up.
Scraping himself to the bathroom.
'Be quick, and don't use all the hot water.'
'Sound.'
Untie the tiny knot in his tie.
Like a peanut.
Says his pal did it for a laugh.
How's that a laugh?
Pack their bags.
Paul's has got a hole in.
It's just bloody new.
'MUM?! Daryll won't get out the shower.'
Daryll.
For God's sake.
Daryll.
Daryll.
He's out.
Paul's in.
Phone Mum.

'I'll take you to your appointment after training.'
'Don't be late.'
'When am I ever late?'
Daryll's in the kitchen now.
'Where's my stuff?'
All here.
Clean.
Pressed.
'Sandwiches, again?'
'Aye.'
'All my pals get money.'
'How much like?'
'£4.'
£4? Whit do they need four quid for? That's £20 a week. £80 a month. A whole day's work. And I'm struggling to breathe. And Paul's like 'Mum, mind that trip I'm meant to be on? Gonnae need a tenner for it.' And he's also piping in about the sandwiches. About how 'they're minging'. I tell them I've got a yogurt as well. And they laugh. At me. And my chest is a wee bit tighter.
Letter on the table.
Red writing.
Big capitals.
Not now.
'You're such a riddy mum.'
'So embarrassing.'
'Probably got us fucking Froobs again.'

All   'HAAAAAHHHHH'

A shift.

Jo (*to audience*)   Training session one.

The B (*to audience*)   First time I've played football in God knows how long.

Lorraine (*to audience*)   Noor's sitting at the side looking at her phone.

Noor (*to audience*)   Lorraine's doing some mad yoga pose.

Lorraine (*to audience*)   Downward dog.

Noor (*to audience*)   Jo's pacing about.

The B (*to audience*)   It's pranging me oot.

Jo (*to audience*)   Because Sammy's late.

Sammy   Sorry. This morning was a nightmare.

Jo   You can't miss training.

The B   Well, she's here now.

Jo   She's late.

The B   You starting like?

Jo   No. Not starting.

Sammy   The bus was late.

Noor   Number 34?

All except **Lorraine**   Useless bloody buses.

Lorraine   Could you not have taken a taxi? Save time?

Jo   Eh?

The B   She's not, like, the Pope or sut-ing!

Jo   Well anyway, you're here now. Just don't let it happen again.

Sammy   Aye, aye, of course.

Jo   Look, if we want to win this tournament, we need to act like pros. We need to all strive to be the first in and last out. Just like Ronaldo.

Lorraine   Is he not a big fatty now?

The B   Nah, he's a beast.

Noor   Aye a pure nonce.

Jo   Naw! Not that kind of beast but . . . eh . . . maybe that kind of beast. But that doesnae matter. And Lorraine, you're talking about the wrong Ronaldo.

Lorraine   Two Ronaldos? How does that work? If only there were two of me.

Sammy   Could probably do with three of me.

The B *starts to kick the goal posts, growl and clap her hands together. Her ritual.*

Jo   Right. Whit is The B doing?

Sammy (*to audience*)   I heard The B was in the Royal Marine Commandos.

Noor (*to audience*)   I heard The B toured with WWE.

Jo (*to audience*)   I heard The B did rugby trials for Scotland U21s – when she was seven.

Lorraine   Is she ok?

Jo   Hard to tell.

Noor   She was at my school and folk says she like murdered her family.

Lorraine   That can't be true. How would she get out?

Noor   A technicality apparently.

Lorraine   Oh my goodness.

Sammy   I'm sure she's lovely.

Lorraine   Are we safe?

The B   Safe fae whit?

All   Nothing.

The B   Tell me.

Noor   It's nothing.

The B   Whit they scared of?

Noor   You . . .

The B   So they fucking should be.

Lorraine (*to audience*)   Coach has been down the other end of the pitch on his phone since we got here.

Sammy (*to audience*)   Looks like it's bad news.

Jo (*to audience*)   Someone's just hung up on him.

Noor (*as* **Coach**)   Right girls. Ready to go? Sorry, I had some important business to deal with there.

Jo (*to audience*)   Messy divorce.

Sammy (*to audience*)   His wife chucked him out.

The B (*to audience*)   He's sleeping in the garage.

Jo   And he comes over and says:

Noor (*as* **Coach**)   Look, today will feel painful and it'll feel even more brutal tomorrow. But that's the point. I hope. We've only got three weeks to get into shape. Let's get a passing drill going. On the white line.

Jo (*to audience*)   I'm aff the white lines. Coach buggers off to put some cones out and I tell everyone about a wee ritual we have here. Something we do before every session and every game to remind us why we're here. It goes like this. (*She shouts at the girls.*) Same team!

The B   Yer fucking shouting down my ear man.

Jo   Say it like you mean it then.

The B   Aye, same team. Noor?

Noor (*quietly*)   Same team.

Jo   Speak up.

The B   Aye this ear's already fucked so might as well even it up.

Noor   Same team!

Jo   That's better.

Sammy   Cannae believe I'm saying this but . . . same team.

Lorraine   And we all put our hands in?

The B   Aye like the hokey cokey, man, just without all the shaking about, ken.

Lorraine   Right, yep.

Lorraine *sticks her hand in lightly.*

Sammy   We're not going to bite.

Lorraine   Oh, ok . . .

The B   Well I might.

Jo   Lorraine?

Lorraine *sticks her hand in properly.*

Lorraine   Same team.

All   Same team.

Blows whistle.

Lorraine (*to audience*)   So we run onto the pitch.

Jo (*to audience*)   Ready to go.

Sammy (*to audience*)   And Noor asks to sit on the side for a bit.

Noor   Gees five and I'll join in.

Jo   Pass and go.

The B   One touch. Pass. Go.

Sammy   One touch. Pass. Go.

Lorraine   One touch. Pass. Go.

Noor *sits out.* **Lorraine** *and* **Jo** *in a pair on one side and* **Sammy** *and* **The B** *together opposite in their own space.* **The B** *makes a mistake.*

The B   FUCK SAKE.

Sammy   Hey, hey, it's alright.

The B   Every fucking time, man. Used to be able to control it in my sleep. Haven't kicked a ball in three year.

Sammy   We're just training. That's what this is all about, practising, getting better.

The B   Frustrating, like.

Sammy   I know. Let's just go again and it'll get easier.

On the other side.

Lorraine   Sorry to ask, but what's Bethany's . . . ehm . . . well?

Jo   Whit?

Lorraine   Well . . . problem?

Jo   Problem?

Lorraine   I mean . . . issue . . . I mean . . . difficulties . . . I mean . . . y'know.

Jo   Right . . . Who?

Lorraine   Bethany.

Jo   Aw, you mean The B.

Lorraine   B?

Jo   Aye, B. The B. I used to play with her years ago before she went inside, back when the sessions were down the fives.

Lorraine   Is she alright?

Jo   She's always been like this.

Lorraine   Must be having a bad day.

Jo   This is her on a good day.

Lorraine   Oh, I see . . . I've never met someone who's been to p-prison before.

Jo   First time for everything, eh?

Lorraine   Well we'll all have earned our glass of Chablis tonight!

Beat.

Jo   Give me a sec.

Jo *goes to* **Noor**.

Jo   What's up?

Noor   Aw, nothing. Just having a rest.

Jo   You've been sat for five minutes, time to get going.

Noor   I don't feel like it.

Jo   That's not an excuse we use around here.

Noor   Do you not just sometimes need a moment?

Jo   Not when it comes to this. We're here to train.

Noor   I know, it's just I like to practise on my own.

Jo   Train hard, win more. Same team. Let's see what you've got.

Noor   I don't –

Jo   There's a dozen other players who would take your spot. If you hang around waiting for things to happen, you'll wake up one day wondering where your life has gone.

Noor   Why do you care so much?

Jo   No reason. You just remind me of someone, that's all. Come on. You can do this.

A shift.

Sammy   Noor! You're brilliant.

The B   Woah, CristiaNoor Ronaldo. Ha ha.

Lorraine   Looks like we have ourselves a decent player.

Jo   Yeah. Looks like it . . .

Sammy   You could play for Dundee!

The B   Or Celtic.

Jo   Why'd you want to play for them?

The B   Forgot you were a big mad hun.

Sammy   Who do you support Lorraine?

Lorraine   My ex supports Hearts. So what's the opposite of Hearts?

The B   Hibs.

Lorraine   They'll do nicely then.

Jo   Enough chatting. Back to work. Pass and go.

The B   One touch. Pass. Go.

Lorraine   One touch. Pass. Go.

Noor   One touch. Pass. Go.

A shift.

Sammy   And I cannae do this. Why me? Why am I here? And I'm thinking about tomorrow's 6am start. No sleep. Out of bed. Wee. Shower. Lunch money. Cold water. Ironing. Embarrassing yogurt. Running through my hair. Onto my skull. Over my face. Eight wee triangles now. Catch my breath. Catch my breath. Catch my breath.

Letter in my pocket.
Red writing.
Big capitals.
EVICTION NOTICE.

Twenty-eight days.

Trip on my laces.

And they're laughing.

Just like my boys.

They're laughing.

All   'HAAAAHHHH'

The whistle goes.

TRAINING SESSION 3

Noor   I've got this teacher at school, right? She's really sound. Teaches art – not just paintings but the history and stuff as well. She says I'm decent but apparently I'm falling behind.

She's always had a soft spot for me because she knows my Nanu and Nana are the only family I've ever had. Everyone thinks your Nana is your Granny and your Nanu is your Grandad. But it's actually the other way round.

Everything's fine by the way. But the reason I'm falling behind is because Nanu died last year. It's fine. I'm fine. It was ages ago. But Nana's not been keeping that well.

I mind when it was the four of us. Me, my big brother Nadeem, Nana and Nanu. The first Saturday of every month Nanu would take us to Glasgow to see our cousins. We'd pick up cassettes that we'd listen to all the way back home in the car. Classics like Kishore Kumar, Lata Mangeshkar and some pure banging Bollywood soundtracks.

Then we would get back at 9pm, sit down and turn on ZEE TV. Watch a three-and-a-half hour Bollywood film.

Three and a half hours is a long time but there'd always be a wee break every fifteen minutes to dash to the toilet and get some snacks. Nanu always made the best rosh malai. She used to make it so sweet, I can still taste it. I've tried to make it but it's never been the same. Won't stop me trying though.

The B (*to audience*)   Noor is with her pals.

Lorraine (*to audience*)   Shiny puffer jackets.

Jo (*to audience*)   Hair slicked back.

Sammy (*to audience*)   Chewing Chuggy.

The B (*to audience*)   Chuggy?

Jo (*to audience*)   I call it chingy.

Noor (*to audience*)   I think you all mean chuddy.

Lorraine, **The B**, **Jo** *and* **Sammy** *become* **Noor**'s *pals*.

Lorraine   Noor! You'll never guess who Jason's going out with now?

Noor   Oh my god who?

Jo   Helen!

Noor   Helen McKiver? Skiver McKiver?

Sammy   Apparently they are going to Furies tonight.

Lorraine   So we're going as well.

The B   Going to be so jokes.

Noor   Tonight? Ah . . . I cannae.

Lorraine   If you want to get in you're going to need to borrow someone's ID. Because the Tipp-Ex trick is fucked now. They're onto us.

Noor   The Tipp-Ex trick?

The B   Aye. You Tipp-Ex over the 6 of your Young Scot card and you draw a 0 where the 6 was.

Sammy   Pure genius like. Curriculum for Excellence shit. Bringing thegether skills fae art and maths.

Jo   What the fuck you talking about?

Lorraine   I'll get my big sister's. She's just got a new boyfriend so she won't be out, eh?

Jo   Aw fuck aye. She's going out with Greg.

Noor   Aye he's a cheating bastard. Wouldn't be letting him out of my sight.

Sammy   Aye I've gave him a handy in the disabled toilets a couple of years ago.

Jo   You've given everyone a fucking handy, even Mr Knight.

Noor   He's a teacher. That's fucked.

The B   He's no a real one. He teaches PE.

Noor   Still a teacher but . . .

Lorraine   What you gonna do, Noor?

Noor   I can't come.

Lorraine   What? You need to come. Everyone is going to be there.

Noor   But nae one looks like me and I cannae anyway.

The B   You scared your mum will give you a row?

Noor   Aye, maybe. I mean . . . Nah. I mean . . .

The whistle goes. Everyone into formation. Ready to go.

Jo   Noor. Back in the room.

Noor   Sorry. What did you say?

Jo   Coach has handed the reins over to me today. Some sort of situation down at the Glasgow pitches.

The B (*to* **Noor**)   So he says.

Lorraine   What's happened?

Jo   Best not to ask, eh?

The B   Aye, mind your own.

Lorraine   Right. Of course.

Jo   Anyway, good few sessions last week, ladies. One week down, two to go. Time for a bit of fun.

Sammy   Fun?

Jo   Aye, fun! We're going to play a little game. Grab a bib and tuck it into the back of your shorts. Last one still with a bib is the winner. Go!

They play the game.

Sammy *is out first. Followed by* **Lorraine** *who sanitises her hands. This distracts* **The B** *and then* **Noor** *puts her out.*

A final showdown between **Jo** *and* **Noor**.

Jo *wins.*

Jo   Better luck next time, eh? Let's take 5 there.

The B *goes straight to her phone.*

The B   Fuuuuuuuuucckkkk.

Sammy   Is everything ok?

The B (*quietly*)   aye.

Lorraine   You don't seem like you're ok.

Jo (*whispering*)   Sssh don't poke the bear.

Lorraine (*whispering*)   I thought she was a bee?

Jo (*whispering*)   Would you poke a fucking bee?!

Sammy *goes over with* **Noor**. **The B**'s *hands are in her head.*

Sammy   Hey B. Are you alright?

The B   I'm fucking fine.

Noor   Ok. But you don't look fine.

Sammy   Is there anything we can do?

The B   Get me a fucking job. Then I'll be alright.

Sammy   I don't think I can. Noor?

Noor   I would if I could but I'm still at school.

The B   Ever been rejected from McDonald's? A new fucking low. They do this personality test. Online. Had to go to the library to do it. And they make you answer all these stupid questions about how trustworthy you are, how patient, how likely you are to lose your shit. And I'm honest, right? Because I pride myself on that. And I just end up looking like a mug. How can you fail a fucking personality test for McDonald's? Have you seen the actual nick of folk that work in McDonald's?

Sammy   If you've served your time you should be able to come out and live your life.

Noor   What do you want to do like?

The B   Eh . . . Well . . . I don't want to sound stupid like.

Sammy   You won't. Ever.

The B   Well . . . like . . . Be a singer.

Noor *laughs.*

The B   Don't you fucking laugh at me. Or I'll kick your wee heid in ya wee shite. You're lucky I even brought you here.

Sammy   She's not laughing. She's just . . . She's just . . . ehmm . . .

Noor   Surprised.

The B   Surprised?

Noor   Aye. Like. I didnae know you sung. So I was just like . . . aye . . . surprised.

Sammy   Sing us a song then?

The B   I only sing for special occasions or if I'm getting paid.

Lorraine   Oh! If we're doing a sing song I've got a few numbers too! I used to be in the church choir.

Jo   You go to church?

Lorraine   Not anymore.

Jo   Me neither. Look, B. Chin up. Put your energy into this training session and you'll feel much better. Let's go.

The five players start an individual training drill.

Lorraine   Ladies? Is there any way we can clean the balls before practice?

The B   Aye, you volunteering?

Lorraine   Well is there not someone else who could . . .?

Sammy   What, clean the balls for us? We're hardly Barcelona!

Noor   We're barely Broughty Ferry!

Jo   We're the Scotland team. Cleaner balls mean higher standards.

Noor *and* **The B** *laugh but* **Jo** *is dead serious.*

Jo   What the fuck yous laughing at? Higher standards mean better performances. I'll speak to Coach.

The B   Lorraine why don't you do it? You no used to big dirty filthy balls like?

Lorraine   I beg your pardon?

Jo   RIGHT. Gather round for a demonstration. I haven't seen a single shot on target all session. Shooting 101. Everyone watching, especially you Sasha.

Noor   Who's Sasha?

Jo   I mean Noor. Noor. Anyway. You place the ball on the spot.

Plant your foot flat on the ground.

And bend your knee as you bring your kicking foot down.

A steady planted foot is crucial.

Remember, you're not just using your legs, it's the whole body.

Breathe.

And strike.

Noor (*mumbles*)   You could maybe do with leaning into it a bit more.

Jo   What?

Noor   Nothing.

Jo   Go on.

Noor   You could maybe do with leaning into it a bit more. You were leaning back.

Jo   Oh very good. You go for it then.

Noor   Nah.

Jo   I wasn't asking.

Noor   I'm fine.

Jo   But I'm the Captain and Coach isn't here so . . .

Noor   So what?

Jo   Do you think you could do this better or something?

Noor   Naw.

Jo   You're up. Hotshot.

A shift.

Sammy (*to audience*)   Noor steps up.

Lorraine (*to audience*)   She's ready.

The B (*to audience*)   She places the ball on the spot.

Lorraine (*to audience*)   Takes a step back.

The B (*to audience*)   Breathes in.

Sammy (*to audience*)   And she stares at the goal.

The B (*to audience*)   She's wee but she looks massive.

Lorraine (*to audience*)   She plants her foot.

Sammy (*to audience*)   Just like Jo said.

Lorraine (*to audience*)   Bends her knee.

Sammy (*to audience*)   Leans right over the ball.

The B (*to audience*)   Just like Noor said.

Sammy (*to audience*)   And the baw takes flight.

The B (*to audience*)   Soars like a fucking meteor.

Lorraine (*to audience*)   She's smashed it.

The B (*to audience*)   Hard as fuck.

Sammy (*to audience*)   Fae her legs.

Lorraine (*to audience*)   Comes pure power.

The B (*to audience*)   Flames coming oot the back of the ball.

Sammy (*to audience*)   Nah there wisnae.

The B (*to audience*)   Aye but imagine there wis.

Lorraine (*to audience*)   And it rockets.

The B (*to audience*)   Thunders.

Sammy (*to audience*)   Hurtles.

The B (*to audience*)   Into the Top Bins.

Lorraine (*to audience*)   The what?

The B (*to audience*)   The top corner.

Lorraine (*to audience*)   Pin-point accuracy.

Sammy (*to audience*)   And we go wild.

All three   YAAAAAASSSSSSSS.

But **Jo** *doesn't react.*

Sammy   Oh my God! I've got five missed calls from Daryll. I've missed their dinner. I thought they were out tonight. I've got to go. I'm sorry.

Jo   Wait! Sammy! We're not finished here!

Sammy   I am.

Jo   Sammy!

A shift.

Lorraine, **The B**, **Jo** *and* **Sammy** *become* **Noor**'s *pals again.*

Lorraine   Oh my god, Noor. I can't believe you weren't there last night. It was a total riot.

Noor   I couldn't get ID. I was busy.

Jo   Busy with what like?

Noor   Just. Like . . . Busy.

Sammy   Rachel said you like lived with your Grandad?

Noor   Nah . . . I just go around there a lot.

The B   Yeah I thought so. Or you'd smell like old people.

Noor   Aye exactly. Rachel is a bitch for saying that like.

Sammy   You like pure have to come on Saturday.

Noor   I totally will.

Jo   We'll come round and get you.

Noor   No. No don't. I'll meet yous there. Maybe I'll try the Tipp-Ex trick.

The pals leave.

Noor   See now? Saturdays aren't the same. I've not seen my cousins in months. No new cassettes. No drive to Glasgow – instead it's cups of tea, cooking dinner and helping Nana with his bath. And by the time it's 9pm, he's already asleep in his chair. I could watch the film myself but it's just not the same.

It started with him forgetting which day it is. But now it's getting worse. Sometimes he thinks she's still here. It would always be songs by folk like Rabindranath Tagore that gave Nana, like, an anchor. But everything's just slipping now and it's getting harder for him. Harder for me. But see this morning? I got the cassettes out and put his song on again. And for the first time in months, he looked at me and smiled. In his eyes, him and Nanu were dancing. And everything felt easier, for three minutes at least.

THE INTERVIEW

We're at a job interview. **Sammy**, **Jo**, **Noor** *and* **Lorraine** *play the panel.*

Lorraine   Thank you for coming in today, Bethany. We appreciate it's short notice but things move very quickly here at Coffee-to-go-go. Always a high turnover of employees, which makes for a fun and invigorating work environment.

The B   Not a problem. I'm extremely delighted to meet you all. I've always been a fan of Coffee to go.

Sammy   Go-go.

The B   Sorry?

Noor   Go-go.

Jo   It's two gos.

Lorraine   Coffee

(*All except* **The B**)   To-go-go.

The B   Aye. My utmost apologies. I've always been a fan of coffee to go go, ever since I was wee.

Lorraine   You must be thinking of a different chain. We're a relatively recent start up, three years into our seventy-five-year strategy. A large amount of growth in a short space of time but that hasn't stopped our social mission either.

Sammy   We do a lot of work in the community.

Noor   A lot of work.

Jo   So much work.

Lorraine   But more about you, Bethany. We want to hear from you. This is a space for you to flourish. Talk us through your recent employment history.

The B   Well you'll ken from my CV about my record.

Sammy   Your record?

Noor   How exciting!

Jo   We love it when high achievers join the team.

The B   I don't think you'd quite call me a high achiever like.

Lorraine   Don't be modest. Coffee-to-go-go is all about people who get up and

(*All except* **The B**)   Go-go.

Jo   Now then, Bethany, first part of the interview. A little bit of role play.

Sammy   I want you to imagine that I'm a customer and you are one of our employees. And that I'm being a bit of a fusspot.

Lorraine   A difficult Daniel.

Noor   She's just purchased a coffee but is claiming that you've short-changed them.

Lorraine   So, in this situation, what do you do?

The B (*jokingly*)   I'd tell them where to fucking go-go. Haha. If you know what I mean.

Jo   But Bethany the customer is always right . . .

The B   They're not right if they are fucking wrong. Why do folk pay 3 quid for a coffee anyway when you can just make it in the hoose? What's the fucking difference?

Lorraine   Let's all just watch our language.

The B   Folk are always telling me to mind my language. Trying to get me to be someone I'm not.

Sammy   I think that might be us for today. Thank you for coming in Bethany.

The B   It's not Bethany. It's The B. And when do I hear back?

Back in the room.

TRAINING SESSION 5

Noor (*to audience*)   So we've got this name for Lorraine now.

Sammy (*to audience*)   The Cat.

The B (*to audience*)   Aye, more like the pussy.

Jo (*to audience*)   Shut up, B.

Noor (*to audience*)   It's the Cat.

Sammy (*to audience*)   On account of her feline-like reflexes.

Jo (*to audience*)   She used to do yoga five times a week.

The B (*to audience*)   When she could afford it.

Noor (*to audience*)   So she's proper bendy and that.

Sammy (*to audience*)   And can fling herself about a bit.

The B (*to audience*)   Like a recoiling spring.

Jo (*to audience*)   She's alright outfield but nothing special.

The B (*to audience*)   Heavy touch and no the best at tracking back.

Jo (*to audience*)   But in goals she's like Seaman.

The B (*to audience*)   Aye a big mad cum bucket.

Lorraine   That's disgusting.

Jo   Nah, David Seaman, Lorraine.

The B (*to audience*)   Ponytail.

Noor (*to audience*)   Big 'tache.

Lorraine   I do not have a moustache.

Jo (*to audience*)   Proper good keeper.

The B (*to audience*)   World class.

Jo (*to audience*)   Screams instructions from the back.

The B (*to audience*)   And makes these impossible saves.

Sammy (*to audience*)   You wouldnae ken it like, I saw her knitting in a break once.

Jo (*to audience*)   But she proper puts her body on the line.

Noor (*to audience*)   We've found her.

Sammy (*to audience*)   Our cat.

TRAINING SESSION 9

Sammy *becomes the* **Coach**.

Sammy (*as* **Coach**)   Right how's everyone feeling today then?

The B   Shite.

Noor   Pish.

Lorraine Inspired.

Jo Pumped.

Lorraine *wipes her seat down with a wet wipe before she sits on it.*
The B *gives her a death stare.*

Sammy (*as* **Coach**)   Well you're all a barrel of laughs today.
Least the waiter in the Holiday Inn doesn't know your name
because you're having to eat your breakfast, lunch and
dinner there. But at least we've had a brilliant three weeks
together, ladies. And all of a sudden, it's our last training
session. So I've brought five of the boys in to play opposite
yous. A warm-up match.

Noor Aw whit!

Jo This'll be good.

Lorraine Are the boys not better than us?

The B Shut your hole Lorraine. Bit of confidence building
eh? Let's be fucking havin yes. Ye bunch of tiny penised
bawbags!!

Lorraine Tiny penised bawbags? Doesn't even make sense.

Sammy (*as* **Coach**)   You'll already know them I'm sure from
being in and around the building, but for introduction's
sake. We've got the team captain – Blair.

Jo (*as* **Blair**)   Alright, ladies, looking lovely as ever.

The B This isnae fucking *Love Island*.

Sammy (*as* **Coach**)   We've got the wee man on the wings,
rocket Robbie.

Noor (*as* **Robbie**)   It's not cause I'm fast. It's cause one
bonfire night I stuck a firework up my –

Sammy (*as* **Coach**)   Too much information Robbie. Next
up, we've got Kenny, they call him the hound dog because
he's like a guard dog in goals.

Lorraine (*as* **Kenny**)   Woof woof.

The B   Call that a bark you wee scroat, I'll show you a bark when we get on the field.

Lorraine *as* **Kenny** *whimpers like a dog.*

Sammy (*as* **Coach**)   And Hulk.

Lorraine   Is that his Christian name?

The B (*as the Hulk*)   It is actually.

Lorraine   But you have a surname?

The B (*as the Hulk*)   Negative. Just Hulk. Like Drake. Or Zendaya.

Sammy (*as* **Coach**)   And finally, silent Simon.

Sammy (*as* **Simon**)   *Silence*

Noor   Alright Simon.

Sammy (*as* **Simon**)   *Silence*

Jo   Simon?

Sammy (*as* **Simon**)   *Silence*

The B   Simon. Simon . . . Simon.

Lorraine   Bit rude. Is he always like that?

The B   Lorraine, what have we said about asking questions?

Sammy (*as* **Coach**)   Let's take ten to warm up then we'll get a match running.

Whistle.

The B   Do you always have to be so rude to folk?

Lorraine   Me rude? Pot calling the kettle black much.

The B   What you on about fucking pots and kettles, man? Stop being so nosy. Keep your neb away from where it don't belong and concentrate on playing a good game.

Lorraine   You're one to speak about manners, Bethany. You have the mouth of a sailor.

The B   Well you have the mouth of a cunt.

Lorraine   I will not sit here and take that language. I'd like to speak to the Change Centre manager.

Noor   Aye, alright Karen.

Lorraine   It's Lorraine.

Noor   Naw, a Karen is a –

A shift.

Lorraine   It's Lorraine. Yes. Well I've been out of work for. Oh. Well. Since I met Jeremy. He didn't . . . I didn't . . . Not seriously for years.

Am I looking?

No not yet, it's been difficult since we –

Separated. Recently, yes. Traded me in for a younger model. Someone at his work. Twenty years younger.

Disability, no. How about a broken heart. Ha. What? No. It was a jo –

Not caring for anyone, just myself.

Children, no. Couldn't have them. Well, Jeremy didn't wan –

No, just the dog. Bichon Frisé.

With my neighbour. So, temporary accommodation. Staying with my neighbour.

No, no savings no.

Oh.

£158.06.

Is that per . . .

Oh per week.

It's just a bit of a . . .

A shock I guess.

How do you . . .?

Or how does one . . .?

I'm used to a bit . . .

Well, more . . .

A shift.

Jo   Lorraine. Listen up.

Lorraine   Sorry, I was miles away.

Sammy   Jo?

Jo   One second, Sammy.

Sammy   But Jo –

Jo   I said one second. We need to all band together to beat these lads.

Sammy   But that's what I'm trying to say –

Jo   Can you just fucking listen to me? One voice. We need to focus tonight. Pull together in the same direction. Let's end training on a high before the tournament. Now, what is it, Sammy?

Sammy   Nothing . . .

Jo   Good. Then let's do this.

Noor (*to audience*)   The boys think they are too good for us like.

Jo (*to audience*)   They start slowly.

The B (*to audience*)   The so-called Rocketman is slow off the mark.

Lorraine (*to audience*) The B nicks the ball.

Sammy (*to audience*) Passes inside to Noor who twists.

Lorraine (*to audience*) Turns.

Sammy (*to audience*) Dances round Blair.

Noor (*to audience*) I play a one-two with Jo.

Lorraine (*to audience*) Beautiful.

Jo (*to audience*) Noor touches it to the side.

Sammy (*to audience*) Once past Hulk.

The B (*to audience*) Twice past Simon.

Lorraine (*to audience*) The space opens up.

Noor (*to audience*) I lay it off for Sammy.

Jo (*to audience*) The moment's perfect.

The B (*to audience*) Sammy hits it and . . .

Noor (*to audience*) The ball skys over the bar.

Lorraine (*to audience*) Half time.

A shift.

Sammy Lean over the ball. I'm supposed to lean over the ball. I know.

Noor Hey it's ok, nobody said anything.

The B Head up Sammy.

Jo You should have put that away.

Sammy I'm not as good as you guys. Plain and simple. It's just I see yous training and I'm trying my hardest I really am but it's too hard. I look forward all day to coming and playing with yous and then I get here and I try my hardest and I'm still rubbish. I'm sorry.

Lorraine There's no need to apologise.

Noor   It's just one chance.

Lorraine   This is a friendly.

The B   And that was a cracking move. I thought Blair had shat himself when you skinned him like that, Noor. And you were class Sammy.

Sammy   I just – I just. Can't do this anymore. It's too much. With all this training. The boys. And Mum, I'll have to move back in with my fucking mum.

Lorraine   What's going on, darling?

Sammy   I got a letter. Have to leave the flat. Another two weeks before I'm out. Then on to the next one. And who knows how long it'll be before I get another letter? And the bairns got locked out last week. Nae dinner out in the cold.

The B   That wasn't your fault. The session ran on.

Sammy   Those boys rely on me and they cannae be cold. They cannae go hungry. They need me. I'm only here because they love football. I thought it'd give us something to talk about. But it's only pushing us further away. They deserve the best. The best me. And so do yous. I quit. I'm sorry.

Everyone kicks off.

Jo   Oi. Give us a minute girls, would you?

Lorraine, **The B** *and* **Noor** *go and get some water.*

Jo   You cannae quit Sammy.

Sammy   But I'm terrible.

Jo   Well – You're . . . eh . . .

Sammy   I'm crap. Just admit it. It will all be easier and I can just go home. You can find another player.

Jo   It's too late now. We leave tomorrow.

Sammy   A new player won't let you down.

Jo   There's only one way you'll ever let us down. And that's if you leave. We're a team. And we've worked so hard. Here, what was your time on the circuits week one?

Sammy   54 seconds.

Jo   And what is it now?

Sammy   Under 35, I think.

Jo   See? Each of us improving everywhere you look. And the girls need you. There's no one else in the team does what you do. We've got skills and stamina covered. That's the easy part. But you give the team something nobody else can.

Sammy   What's that?

Jo   Heart. You care. You make us all care. And we can't win without it.

Sammy   You mean that?

Jo   I mean it. And by the way, they can help you out with housing stuff upstairs. They were proper on it when my foster family kicked me out.

Sammy   Sorry to hear that, Jo.

Jo   Make sure you speak to them after the session. Now let's go out there and win.

Back to the game.

Lorraine (*to audience*)   The boys start better.

The B (*to audience*)   Fired up because.

All   'We cannae get beaten by a bunch of girls.'

The B (*to audience*)   Fannies.

Noor (*to audience*)   Hulk powers through a tackle.

Jo (*to audience*)   Blair dribbles through the midfield like there's no one there.

Sammy (*to audience*)   Rocketman cuts inside to take a shot . . .

Noor (*to audience*)   But The B is there.

The B (*to audience*)   Blocks.

Sammy (*to audience*)   And Lorraine pounces on the loose ball in the box.

All (*to audience*)   The Cat.

The B (*to audience*)   Passes out to Noor who skins Simon.

Lorraine (*to audience*)   Sammy has the ball now.

Jo (*to audience*)   Running with pace.

The B (*to audience*)   Fire in her eyes.

Noor (*to audience*)   Ice in her veins.

Lorraine (*to audience*)   She sees an opening.

Jo (*to audience*)   Leans over the ball.

Noor (*to audience*)   And plays a pure inch-perfect pass.

The B (*to audience*)   To Jo who takes one touch before . . .

All   GOOOOAAAAAALLLLLLL

Audience encouraged to celebrate.

Jo   Better luck next time, boys!

Sammy   Unbelievable.

Jo   Good job, Sammy.

Noor   Aye, what a ball.

Sammy   Team effort.

Lorraine   How about a wee glass of fizz to celebrate?

The B   Read the fucking room.

Jo   Fourteen months clean and sober. Can if yous want.

Lorraine   Oh . . . sorry, Jo. Well played everyone. Buzzing for this tournament.

Lorraine *sanitises her hands.*

The B   Buzzing, aye?

Lorraine   Yeah isn't that what you lot always say?

The B   Us lot? Thought we were a team? Or are we too dirty for that?

Lorraine   No, I do not think you're dirty.

The B   People like you usually stay clear of the Change Centre and maybe that's for the best eh?

Lorraine   Maybe I don't have a choice, did you think about that?

The B   If you don't want to be here then you can fuck off.

Lorraine   I want to be here.

The B   Well what's with the cleaning the balls, and wiping seats and fucking hand sanitiser and that then. Covid's over.

Lorraine   Well it's not but –

The B   But what?

Lorraine   I –

The B   But fucking what?

Lorraine   Keeping things clean and in order is one of the few things I can control right now. My whole life's been turned upside down. Stupid bloody Jeremy and his slapper of a secretary. I used to be normal. Now I obsessively check the hob, flick the switches seven times before bed, don't stand on the cracks on the pavement. Football. This team. Are the only things in my life that help me keep my mind off the rest of the shit.

The B   Fucking hell. She's more mental than me.

Noor   Don't know about that like.

The B   Shut it wee baws.

They laugh.

Jo   Look girls. We leave for the tournament tomorrow. We're nearly there.

I need you ladies.

I need you to win.

This is your last chance. You're either doing this or you're not. What do you say?

Jo *puts her arm in.*

Jo   Same team.

Noor *puts her arm in.*

Noor   Same team

Sammy *takes a deep breath and puts her arm in.*

Sammy   Same team!

Lorraine *and* **The B** *eye each other up.*

The B   Same team, man.

Lorraine   Same team.

All with their arm in.

All   SAME TEAM.

THE JOURNEY BEGINS

Jo (*to audience*)   The journey begins.

Sammy (*to audience*)   A whole week in Milan.

Lorraine   A holiday, finally. I thought this day would never come.

Jo   This is no holiday. We're going to win.

The B   First time out of Scotland.

Sammy   First time I've left the boys.

Noor   First time I've been on a plane.

The B   Me too, you stick with me.

Lorraine   Well I've flown to New York, Spain, France, Germany, Portugal –

The B   Right easy, fucking Christopher Columbo.

Jo   I buy a big bag from Sports Direct especially.

Lorraine   I fetch two old suitcases and open them on the bed.

The B   I've got like nae stuff still so I just take a bag for life.

Sammy   Daryll! You've used all the towels.

Noor   I put a photo of Nanu and Nana on top of my clothes, pride of place.

Sammy   Paul! Where's the suncream?

The B   I had to fill out all these forms with the guys at the Centre. Was shitting it. Thought I wouldnae be able go. Be another fucking rejection. Didn't get the email right up to the wire but I can come. And it's nice like. Nice to fill out a form and get the chance. The opportunity. To do something. And no want to headbutt someone in the fucking process.

Jo   I put all my clothes for the big occasion in my bag. They told me to pack something nice. I mind when I went to the primary school dance when I was wee. Kicked and screamed about wearing this dress my foster mum bought me for my first holy communion. In the end I wore it. Just to the bus stop though. Dived behind the bush, chucked my trackies on, total 90s, and pulled over my Rangers top. Looked class. Serving the same look tonight. Twenty years later. In Milan.

Lorraine   I hand over half of what I get in my weekly payment to my neighbour who I'm staying with for rent. I'll worry about next week when I'm back. I close the front door and over the road I see her, twenty years younger, going into my house. My old house. Jeremy holding the door for her. I remember when I was treated like that. When that was my life.

This tournament is that wee bit of hope I've been looking for. I'm leaving Lorraine in Scotland. For the next week . . . I am Il Gatto. That's Italian for the Cat.

Noor   Nadeem is taking holidays from work so he can look after Nana. I've told him everything. I've written out instructions on how to work the oven, the shower and the boiler just in case. It's like if he'd ever bothered to help before then it would be easier now. Funny that. I show Nadeem Nanu's favourite Rabindranath Tagore cassette. If he breaks it I'll fucking kill him.

I tell him to phone me, if there's anything at all. To phone me. He tells me it's only a week and I'll be back before I know it.

I'm at the terminal. I see Coach. Big smiley face. Holding a bit of paper with Street Soccer written on it. Like a mad limo driver in a film.

Ping.

Lorraine *becomes one of the girls.*

Lorraine   Where are you? It's Below Deck night. Pizza's on the way xoxo.

Noor   The girls.

Another ping.

The B *becomes* **Nadeem**.

The B   Nana's had a wee accident. Everything's fine though. How do I work the oven again?

Noor   Nadeem.

Naw . . . I can't do this.

I turn around.

I'm getting out of here.

I pick up the pace.

Like I'm through on goal.

The B   Where the fuck are you gawn?

Lorraine   Oh hi, Noor. I just got some new sunnies. Do you like them? I'm so excited. Are you? You must be.

Jo   I thought you had nae money.

Sammy   Are you ok?

Noor   Aye. Eh. Well. Nah, no really. I don't think I can come.

Sammy   You're here now.

Jo   We're going to the World Cup!

Noor   It's all getting a bit much for me like.

The B   Whit?

Lorraine   You're our star player.

Jo   Well I don't know about that.

Sammy   What's up, Noor?

Noor   Ehm . . . It's my pals. Aye . . . my pals and that. I don't want to miss out.

The B   We're your fucking pals.

Lorraine   It's only a week pet.

Noor   Well I'm missing hanging out with them and that. And eh . . . well . . . . My . . .

Jo   Your?

Lorraine   What?

Sammy   If you don't want to talk just now, you don't need to.

The B   Go on. Tell them.

Noor   Well it's my Nana.

The B   He's got that auld timer's disease.

Lorraine   B, do you mean Alzheimer's?

Noor   Aye, dementia. I've never left him before. My brother's looking after him but he's useless. Absolutely useless.

Sammy   I can get Darryl to pop in to make sure everything's alright?

Noor   You'd do that?

Sammy   Of course. We're a family.

Jo   We're team mates, but aye.

Noor   What will I tell the girls?

The B   That you've got nits.

Noor   Nits?

The B   Nits. Works every time.

The plane.

Jo (*as air hostess*)   Ladies and gentlemen the captain has switched on the fasten your seatbelts sign. We ask that you please fasten your seatbelts at this time and secure all baggage underneath your seat or in the overhead compartments.

The B   Oh my god. Oh my god. This turbulence is doing affy things to my stomach like.

Lorraine   Bethany, we're only taxiing to the runway.

Sammy (*to audience*)   We take off.

Noor (*to audience*)   And it's not long before . . .

All   Dooft.

Jo (*to audience*)   We touch down.

The B   Thank God. That was quick.

Jo   We're only in Dublin.

The B   Oh.

Jo   We've still got one more flight to go.

The B   Fuck sake.

Lorraine   Why is it we're not flying direct again?

Jo   Because we're not made of money.

The B   Aye, we're not fucking Elon John.

Noor   Do you mean Elton John?

Lorraine   Or Elon Musk?

The B   Fuck off.

Sammy (*to audience*)   Three hours to wait.

Lorraine (*to audience*)   Sammy's buying postcards to send to back home.

Sammy   I know we're going to Milan and they say 'l love Dublin' but the boys will like them.

The B   The boys won't give a fuck.

Jo (*to audience*)   Board another plane.

Noor (*to audience*)   Three hours.

Jo   Excuse me, could you put your seat up? It's just my legs, I'm playing a big match tomorrow. I'm playing at the World Cup.

Noor (*as passenger*)   Aye, aye. So you are.

All   Dooft.

They arrive in Milan.

TOUCHDOWN IN MILAN

Sammy (*to audience*)   Touchdown in Milan.

The B (*to audience*)   At the border patrol this big Al Pacino lookalike stares at my passport for what feels like fucking thirty minutes then eyeballs me as if I'm a member of the fucking mafia.

Noor (*to audience*)   I heard The B fought in the ice cream wars.

Lorraine (*to audience* I heard The B's nickname in prison was the Godmother.

Jo (*to audience* I heard The B's second name is Soprano and she can only be reached by payphone or a five-hour sit-down lunch.

The B (*to audience*)   Finally Pacino waves me through – all his guys stare at me as I pass. Fucking got me on edge like. They don't know me. They don't know anything about me. A wee mark next to my name and everyone thinks they fucking know me.

Outside.

The B   Oh ya fucker. It's hot.

Jo   Aye, maybe too hot.

Noor   How we meant to play in this?

Sammy   Right. Who needs sunscreen?

Lorraine   Perfetto. Brillante. Eccellente.

The B   Is she having a stroke?

Lorraine   No I'm not having a stroke.

Jo   Do we need to turn you on and off again?

Lorraine   I'm just testing out the local language.

Sammy   Everybody knows Scottish in Europe anyway.

Noor   English.

Sammy   Same thing.

The B   No it's naw.

Lorraine   Will we have time in the itinerary to visit the cathedral?

The B   Aye same time we're going to meet Leonardo DiCaprio ya fud.

Lorraine   He's American . . .

The B   Naw he invented flying and drew naked men.

Lorraine   Right . . .

Jo   We're here to play football.

Sammy (*to audience*)   Lorraine's got this wee book her pal she's staying with gave her.

Noor (*to audience*)   And she's pure rattling off jokes and facts out of it.

Lorraine   Oh, oh, here's one! Listen. Words can't *espresso* how much it means to be here . . . Ha.

The B   Oh Christ . . .

Noor   That's stinking.

Jo   Right. Bus is here. Let's get going ladies. Focus up.

In the bus.

Lorraine   Did you know the Milanese invented the concept of *aperitivo*?

Jo   Alright.

Lorraine   I often say it's not just a drink, it's a lifestyle – one I wholeheartedly embrace!

The B   This book is doing my pan in.

Noor (*to audience*)   The countryside starts turning to brick.

Lorraine (*to audience*)   And we're getting closer to the tournament.

Jo (*to audience*)   What this has all been leading up to.

Sammy (*to audience*)   But for The B we're getting further away.

Noor (*to audience*)   Further away from the tiny room she was in for months.

Sammy (*to audience*)   Naw, years.

Jo (*to audience*)   And something shifts in her.

Lorraine (*to audience*)   She looks lighter somehow.

Noor (*to audience*)   Like, calm.

Sammy (*to audience*)   Well no calm but you ken what I mean?

Jo (*to audience*)   Just different.

A shift.

Lorraine   Did you know 'The Last Supper' is in Milan?

Noor   Aye, in the Santa Maria delle Grazie.

Lorraine   Top marks for you sweetie.

Jo   How do you ken that?

Noor   Art at school.

The B   What is 'The Last Supper'?

Lorraine   One of the greatest masterpieces of the Renaissance era.

Jo   The one with the dinner that Jesus had where all his pals stabbed him in the back.

The B   Sound.

A shift.

Jo (*to audience*)   We arrive at the opening ceremony.

All   Dooft.

Sammy (*to audience*)   In somewhere called the San Siro.

Lorraine (*to audience*)   Which my book says is home to two of the world's most famous football clubs.

Noor (*to audience*)   AC Milan and Inter Milan.

Lorraine (*to audience*)   Although they are rivals, both teams play there.

Noor   Mental, eh?

The B   Aye, imagine Rangers and Celtic both playing at Celtic Park.

Jo   They'd probably have to rename it like.

Someone starts singing 'Nessun Dorma' in the distance.

Noor (*to audience*)   That's when we see them.

Lorraine (*to audience*)   The other players in the tournament.

Sammy (*to audience*)   All in their matching tracksuits.

The B (*to audience*)   Celebrating being here.

Jo (*to audience*)   Together.

Lorraine (*to audience*)   Each nation with their arms around each other singing the same song

Noor (*to audience*)   Together.

Jo (*to audience*)   Naebody kens the words.

Lorraine (*to audience*)   But that doesn't matter.

The B (*to audience*)   Everyone's just singing the tune.

Noor (*to audience*)   It's the feeling that matters.

Jo (*to audience*)   The emotion underpinning everything.

The B (*to audience*)   Some folks over there are crying.

Sammy (*to audience*)   I'm crying!

Lorraine (*to audience*)   The room is filled with hundreds of people creating a volume of sound.

Sammy (*to audience*)   Swelling into one booming voice.

Jo (*to audience*)   We did it. We're here.

They sing 'Nessun Dorma'.

It fills the space.

Half time, if required. Time for your pie, pint or Bovril. I'm sure the manager will give the players a stern talking to and we can expect a better second half than what we've had in the first.

GROUP STAGE

Jo (*to audience*)   So Coach, gets us together.

Sammy (*to audience*)   Into a wee huddle.

The B (*to audience*)   Like Celtic do.

Jo (*to audience*)   Which I'm no that keen on but I do it anyway.

Noor (*to audience*)   And he's like . . .

Lorraine (*as* **Coach**)   We did it. You're here. Representing your country.

The B (*as* **Coach**)   Be prepared to feel the true power of teamwork and community.

Sammy (**as Coach**)   A life-changing moment. Where people who once felt invisible are given a global stage.

Noor (*as* **Coach**)   This pride will last a lifetime. It's the reason I'm here now. Talking to yous. I've done this. Been through it all. But now, it's your turn.

Jo (*as* **Coach**)   I remember every single one of you when you first came down the centre. And it's been amazing to be on this journey with you here.

Lorraine (*as* **Coach**)   Enjoy every minute of it. Please. Every touch. Every pass. Every tackle. For me.

Sammy (*as* **Coach**)   This team's history is waiting to be written. Is still waiting to be written. What will you write?

The B (*as* **Coach**)   Dare you write your names on that page?

Jo (*as* **Coach**)   The World Cup is here. Now let's see what you've got.

Noor (*as* **Coach**)   Show these other countries what Scotland is made of.

Lorraine (*as* **Coach**)   What you are made of.

The B (*as* **Coach**)   No Scotland. No party.

Audience are encouraged to chant 'USA!'

USA.
USA.
USA.
USA.

Sammy   I thought folk only did that in films.

Noor   Aye, it's pure cringe like.

Jo   We just need to focus on us. That's all that matters.

Noor   USA have all the gear.

Sammy   Paint on their faces.

Lorraine   Kitted out head to toe in Nike.

The B *is kicking the posts and growling, again!*

Jo   At least The B is in the zone. You ready Lorraine?

Lorraine   I think so . . . there's nothing in the guidebook about this.

Lorraine *blesses herself.*

Jo   What you doing that for like?

Lorraine   It's my pre game ritual.

Jo   God doesn't exist and even if he did he wouldn't be watching the Homeless World Cup.

Lorraine   But this helps . . .

Jo   We've done our prep. Trust it.

For each game there is a commentator.

The first is **Roberto Baggio**.

The B *plays* **Baggio** *with her Scottish accent.*

The B (*as* **Baggio**)   Ciao and welcome to Sky Sports Italia, I am Roberto Baggio or you might know me as Il Divin Codino: The Divine Ponytail.

Noor   B, I think he was Italian?

The B   I'm naw daeing that and making a pure tit of maself.

Noor   Go on.

The B (*as* **Baggio**)   We are live with Nazionale Solidale. It is the group stage of the Homeless World Cup in Milan and it's a liiiiiive! Our first match . . . it's Scotland versus the United States of America.

USA.
USA.
USA.
USA.

The B (*to audience*)   And we're off.

Noor (*to audience*)   Some American lassie that looks a wee bit like a cross between Gwyneth Paltrow and Jimmy Carr takes the ball and goes on this mad dribble

The B (*to audience*)   Zips right past Noor.

Noor (*to audience*)   Inside The B.

Jo (*to audience*)   Then right down the side.

The B (*to audience*)   And slots one home for the USA.

Lorraine (*to audience*)   And the crowd goes wild.

Sammy   1 – 0 in thirty seconds.

Jo   You're all totally fucking sleeping.

Noor (*to audience*)   Another one.

Sammy (*to audience*)   Another one.

Lorraine (*to audience*)   And almost another one.

The B   We'rc fucking shite.

Jo (*to audience*)   And the whistle goes, again.

A shift.

The B   Thank fuck for that.

Noor   3 – 0 down at half time.

Jo   What was the fucking point in coming? Weeks of training down the drain.

Sammy   Come on Jo, it's not over yet. We've got this, ladies. I've given up a lot to be here. And I've not come all this way for everyone to give up on the first game. Look, I'm scared. All this terrifies me. But you guys make me feel strong. Like I'm meant to be here. So let's lift our heads up, and do what we came here to do.

Noor   Our best.

Lorraine   Prove ourselves.

Jo   Win.

The B   Some speech, Sammy.

Jo   Let's go.

A shift.

Sammy (*to audience*)   Back on the pitch.

Noor (*to audience*)   Jimmy Paltrow gets down the line.

Jo (*to audience*)   Past Noor, again.

Lorraine (*to audience*)   On the inside of The B, again.

Sammy (*to audience*)   She hits the ball and it flies towards the top corner, again.

The B   Aw naw.

Noor (*to audience*)   But something is flying through the air . . .

Sammy (*to audience*)   Is it a bird?

Jo (*to audience*)   Is it a plane?

The B (*to audience*)   No it's . . .

Noor (*to audience*)   The Cat.

The B (*to audience*)   The Cat flies through the air and claws at it.

Jo (*to audience*)   Pounces on it.

Sammy (*to audience*)   Incredible save.

Noor (*to audience*)   But that's not enough.

Jo (*to audience*)   She has a wee look.

Noor (*to audience*)   Rolls it quickly out to Sammy.

Sammy (*to audience*)   I pass it to The B.

The B (*to audience*)   I pass it to Jo.

Noor (*to audience*) Jo puts the ball through a USA player's legs.

Lorraine 'Dude that was totally awesome!'

Jo (*to audience*) I see Noor. She's screaming for it. But I keep going.

Sammy (*to audience*) A brilliant run.

Lorraine (*to audience*) Deftly gliding into space.

Noor (*to audience*) On the edge of the box.

The B (*to audience*) Doesn't even need to look . . .

All GOOOAAAAAALLLLLL!

A shift.

We're outside a gelataria.

Lorraine What a comeback.

Sammy 4–3!

Jo *enters.*

Jo What you's eating?

Lorraine Cones.

Jo We've got a big match later.

Sammy It's only vanilla.

Jo And what the hell is that, Lorraine?

Lorraine A Biscoff gelato with a flake and toffee sauce.

Sammy What is a gelato?

Jo The fuck's a Biscoff more like?

Lorraine The wee biscuits you get in a posh café with your coffee.

Jo I thought you were skint, Lorraine.

Lorraine   No. Well . . . kind of. Well, yes. Everyone's skint these days. I know I shouldn't but it's hard.

Jo   It's hard the other way for me.

Sammy   What do you mean, Jo?

Jo   To spend and that like.

Lorraine   It's easy.

Jo   Every penny I had I used to . . .

Lorraine   Go and get yourself a cone, hen. My treat.

Jo   Can I get a Lucozade instead? Big match and that.

Lorraine   Here, take this.

Jo *takes* **Lorraine***'s card and exits.*

Lorraine   Two scoops in a cone. Jeremy would never have let me have two scoops in a cone.

Sammy   We're celebrating.

Lorraine   He never let me have anything. Shouldn't have been surprised when I was left without a roof over my head.

Sammy   Surely you're entitled to something?

Lorraine   I wouldn't know where to start.

Sammy   You should get a lawyer.

Lorraine   I don't know. But it's you that we should be worrying about. How long are you and the boys going to be at your mum's for?

Sammy   Just as a stopgap. Until I get things sorted.

Lorraine   It'll be nice to have some quality time together.

Sammy   I doubt it. It's just what she's been bloody waiting for. Me to mess up. Again.

Lorraine   But you're an amazing mum.

Sammy She always thought I threw my life away having them so young.

Lorraine People get pregnant. It happens.

Sammy She'll be packing up the place, right now. I said I'd do it when I get back. I'll still have a few days. She thinks I'm incapable. Incapable of doing it myself. But look at me. I'm at the World Cup.

Lorraine And they seem like good boys.

Sammy You think so?

Lorraine They're good boys.

Jo *re-enters without her Lucozade.*

Jo Lorraine . . . your card's been declined?

A shift.

The B (*as* **Baggio**) Ciao. It's time for the second match of the group stages. Scotland vs the Netherlands . . . and it's a liiiiiiive!

Lorraine (*to audience*) Noor immediately skins one.

The B (*to audience*) The crowd go 'oooh'.

(*Ooh*)

That was shite. Let's do it again . . .

The crowd go 'oooh'.

(*Ooooooh*)

Lorraine (*to audience*) Skins two.

(*Oooooooooh*)

Sammy (*to audience*) Then three!

(*Ooooooooooooooooh*)

The B She's balletic out there.

Lorraine   The whole team out cold.

Jo   Show off.

Noor   I look at The B. And we're back at the bus stop.

And they're back in Dundee at a bus stop.

The B   What you watching?

Noor   Mind your own.

The B   Sound. You dinnae recognise me, eh?

Noor   Should I?

The B   Three years away from everything and every cunt forgets you.

Noor   Oh shit. Bethany? I mean B. The B.

The B   Why you flinching?

Noor   No reason. It's just you're quite . . . well . . .

The B   What?

Noor   We'll we've never really talked apart from that time you chucked my school bag in the bin and called me a gimp. And oh when you set fire to my pal's hair for a laugh. And also, more importantly, I thought you were in prison.

The B   I was.

Noor   Everyone says you like murdered your family?

The B   Well I'm here now.

Noor   You've not escaped, have you?

The B   Aye . . . Nah. And even if I had why would I tell you? You a grass or something?

Noor   I'm naw a grass.

The B   You better not be.

Noor   So you just got out?

The B   Yep. Today. Just back in toon. Fresh from Her
Majesty's finest.

Noor   It's His Majesty's now.

The B   Right, I ken The Queen's dead. I've not been asleep
for three year.

Noor   Aye, course. Sorry.

The B   Should you not be at school?

Noor   I'm on my way in. I have, eh, other responsibilities
sometimes.

The B   What were you crying for anyway?

Noor   It's nothing.

The B   Tell me and I won't kick fuck out ye.

Noor   It's my Grandad.

The B   Your Nana?

Noor   You remembered.

The B   Aye. He fucking touching you up like?

Noor   No, no the opposite.

The B   Opposite? You touching him up?

Noor   Naw. My Nanu's naw about anymore. So everything's
kind of a lot. And my Nana's, erm . . .

The B   Your other responsibilities?

Noor   Aye. My brother was meant to look after him today
but he's having to work longer hours because we can't make
the rent. If it keeps going on we're going to get chucked out
and –

The B   – Got you. Here, I don't know if this is your thing
but you know the Lynch Centre up by the big Tesco?

Noor   Course.

The B   They've renamed it the Change Centre, got a proper good reputation and that. A place where people treat you as people. Sounds a bit like a fucking Monkhouse to me but –

Noor   Do you mean where monks live?

The B   Aye, a Monkhouse. Point is. There's loads going on like fitba, Zumba, loads of shite and I remember you were always a good player. The best player, actually if memory serves. I'm going tonight. There's trials on for my old team. You should come along too.

Noor   I'm alright.

The B   You've got to make time for yourself. For up here. (*Points to head.*) Take it from me.

Noor   What, you feel sad sometimes?

The B   Aye, it's shite when every cunt's scared of you.

Noor   Have you seen your brother or sister since you got out?

The B   Not allowed to. Not yet. Will I see you tonight?

Noor   Aye. Maybe.

A shift.

The B   And I look at Noor. We're back in the game now. She's just skinned four folk.

Jo   I'm on the left shouting for the ball. Screaming. Noor. Pass. Noor! Over here.

Noor   I fake a pass to Jo because B's in a better position, wee backheel and she's through on goal.

The B   I've got a nosebleed being this far up the pitch like, but I take a touch and slot it home into bottom corner.

Noor   She roars like a bear.

Jo   And the buzzer goes . . .

The B *and* **Noor** *do an awkward half fist pump half chest pump. But don't care.* **Jo** *is fuming that* **Noor** *didn't pass.*

This team is rocking and rolling. With a bit of jazz.

A shift.

Sammy *is on the phone to* **Daryll** *back home.*

Sammy   I know Daryll but I'm in Italy, what do you want me to do? Well if the controller cable is broken go buy a new one. I left you money. What do you mean it's all gone? Well maybe you should have thought about managing the money better in case things like this happen. I did try and tell you. I don't care what Gran says, I'm your Mum. Hiy stop shouting, how am I supposed to know they are incompatible? Share Paul's laptop for a week then. (*Holds phone away from her ear cause* **Daryll** *is shouting so loudly.*) WELL YOU KNOW WHAT, IF YOU'RE GOING TO BE LIKE THAT, SORT IT OUT YOURSELF.

A shift.

Lorraine (*to audience*)   It's the Belgium game.

The B (*to audience*)   And Sammy is on one.

Noor (*to audience*)   Flying into tackles like she's The B.

The B (*to audience*)   Dribbling down the wings like she's Noor.

Jo (*to audience*)   Firing shots like she's . . . me. Except, she keeps missing.

Lorraine (*to audience*)   She's trying almost too hard.

Noor (*to audience*)   She's thinking about PlayStation controllers and eviction notices.

Jo (*to audience*)   One of her shots canons off the Belgium B.

Lorraine (*to audience*)   As we are calling her.

Sammy (*to audience*)   Cause she's scary.

Noor (*to audience*)   Venomous.

Lorraine (*to audience*)   Lethal.

The B   Alright, fucking hell!

Jo (*to audience*)   The Belgium B tries to intercept.

Sammy (*to audience*)   But Jo is too quick for her.

Lorraine (*to audience*)   She smashes the loose ball through the legs of the keeper.

Sammy (*to audience*)   And the final whistle goes.

The B (*as* **Baggio**)   The Scottish haven't had this much success since they invented the television. Splendidado scenes.

A shift.

Noor   I'm well proud of us!

Sammy   Me too.

Lorraine   I've only conceded six goals the entire tournament!

The B   Well done out there. Who knew a Cat and a B could be pals eh?

Lorraine   I always knew we could be friends.

The B   I said pals. Let's not get carried away like.

Jo   We're playing well.

Sammy   Yeah you are all so good.

Noor   Hiy – and you.

Sammy *shrugs.*

Jo   It's only three games. Nothing's won yet.

The B   We're into the quarter-finals.

Everyone looks at her. Disappointed.

Jo   But . . . I have to say . . . yous are absolutely smashing it out the park.

All   Waaaaay!

The B   Right, who's next?

Jo   Mexico.

All   Aw fuck.

QUARTER-FINAL

Mexican wave. And again but faster and twice round.

Baggio *is back with the guest commentator,* **Graeme Souness***.*

The B (*as* **Baggio**)   It's half time in the Quarter-Final. Scotland 0, Mexico 0. And I'm joined live with Graeme Souness.

Jo   Rangers legend.

Sammy   Dour prick.

Noor   Aye, face like a skelped arse.

Lorraine (*as* **Souness**)   We cannot go on like this. For me, look, it's been a decent run for Scotland but this is surely where their run will end. Their performance today has been an absolute joke.

What are you looking at me like that for? You not agreeing with me.

The B (*as* **Baggio**)   I was just wondering if they agree with you?

Lorraine (*as* **Souness**)   It's the way you looked.

The B (*as* **Baggio**)   I was just saying –

Lorraine (*as* **Souness**)   I'm talking. Mexico, last year's winners, are the most successful team in the history of the Women's World Cup. And for me, today this Scotland team have only got themselves to blame.

A shift.

Jo   I cannae get anywhere near the ball.

Noor   Aye their defence is like a brick wall or something.

Jo   So fucking frustrating.

Lorraine   They've obviously been watching us. They're marking our best scorers. No offence B and Sammy.

The B   None taken.

Sammy   I'm doing my best.

Lorraine   B, you're doing a sterling job at the back. They've barely been able to get a solid shot into me.

The B   Some team, eh?

They fist pump.

Lorraine   So that leaves you Sammy.

Sammy   Sorry. I've been rubbish. Crap actually, maybe I should just –

Lorraine   No. Never apologise darling. That's your superpower.

Sammy   What are you on about?

Lorraine   No one expects you to score.

Sammy   Jeez, thanks, Lorraine.

The B   She's actually right for once.

Jo   No one's marking you.

Noor   You've got bags of space.

The B   Because they think you're shite, Sammy.

Noor   B?!

Lorraine   I guess what we're trying to say is . . .

The B   No one is going to bother marking you because you're the fucking worst player on the pitch.

All (*bar* **The B**)   B!!!

The B   What?

A shift.

The B (*to audience*)   The stadium is quiet.

Noor (*to audience*)   Quieter than it's ever been.

Lorraine (*to audience*)   The tension is palpable.

Sammy (*to audience*)   The Cat rolls the ball out to the B.

Jo (*to audience*)   A Mexican player tries to tackle her.

Noor (*to audience*)   But The B is too strong.

The B (*to audience*)   The Mexican bounces off me like a beach ball.

Jo (*to audience*)   The B passes outside to Noor.

Lorraine (*to audience*)   Noor, now, in a great position in the centre of the pitch.

Sammy (*to audience*)   I'm on her right.

Jo (*to audience*)   I'm on the left.

Lorraine (*to audience*)   The Mexican players swarm around Jo thinking she'll be the target.

Noor (*to audience*)   Leaving Sammy completely free.

The B (*to audience*)   Noor plays a clever pass out to Sammy.

Jo (*to audience*)   Sammy takes a touch.

Noor (*to audience*)   Leans over the ball . . .

The B (*to audience*)   And fires it into the top bins.

All   GOOOOOOOOOAAAAAAAAALL!

'Poznan' backwards bouncing celebration.

Noor   Sammy, you legend!

Lorraine   Just brilliant.

The B   A Sammy smasher.

Jo   I didnae think it was going to work but yous were right.

Sammy   Look at my hands – I can't stop shaking. What just happened? What just happened!

Group hug. **Sammy** *checks her phone.*

Sammy   Voice note from Daryll.

The B   Back down to earth with a bang eh?

Noor (*as* **Darryl**)   Hiya Mum, it's Daryll. Just wanted to say that, like, Paul and I are dead proud of you. We watched the game on the YouTube stream on Paul's laptop and, aye, you were amazing Mum. Just wanted to, like, send our love and that ken.

Sammy *melts.*

THE LAST SUPPER

Jo   I thought it was a painting.

Noor   Aye, it is. Just on the wall.

Jo   We'd get in trouble if we did that.

Noor   What?

Jo   Paint on walls.

Noor   Just enjoy it.

Jo   And it was a bump to get in.

Noor   I know but this is history. Look at it.

Jo   S'pose it is pretty . . . biblical.

Noor   Everyone thinks it's just about Jesus' last supper, but there's loads of hidden meanings and that.

Jo Told ye's. Everyone's scheming against him. Price of being a leader like. Why'd you care about all this pish?

Noor Had a sound teacher. But now I just don't have the time.

Jo Make time.

Noor When I'm no with Nana, I'm training and when I'm no training I'm with the girls.

Jo Listen, you've just got to put yourself first. That's what I do.

Noor Put myself first. Right. Ok. How'd you get into all this? Like, football. Being a captain and that?

Jo Whenever I've been at my worst, there's always been football. It's my way of sticking it to everyone who said I wouldn't make something of my life.

Noor Who said that?

Jo Family. Most of my friends. Everyone. Apart from . . .

Noor Who?

Jo Sasha.

Noor Who's Sasha?

Jo The last person I knew who could kick a ball as well as you.

Noor She must have been quality.

Jo Don't get cheeky like.

Noor Thanks though.

They stare at the painting.

Jo This isn't my history.

Noor It's not mine either.

Jo   We had a history but it was taken away from us. See all this shouting about women's football and stuff? 100 years too late, man.

Noor   What you on about?

Jo   It was equal back in the day. Same quality. Same amount of folk going to games. But the men didn't like that women had just as good a thing as them. Course they didn't. Pricks. So what did the men do? They shut it down. Banned it.

Noor   Banned it?

Jo   Fucking disgraceful, eh? And that's the reason folk chant for John McGinn and Andy Robertson instead of me and you.

Noor   Who's, who?

Jo   Well, who's better?

They smile.

Noor   Both decent in their own ways.

Jo   You'd be even better if you learnt how to pass.

Noor   Ha, coming from you . . .

The B *enters. Looks at the painting.*

The B   Is that it?

SEMI-FINAL

The commentator is **Ally McCoist**. **The B** *is back again as* **Baggio**.

The B (*as* **Baggio**)   Ciao. It's the the semi-final of the Homeless World Cup and I'm delighted to be joined by Ally McCoist.

Jo   Rangers legend.

The B   There's a fucking theme here.

Lorraine   Same team.

Noor   Good one.

Sammy   What does Ally McCoist sound like?

The B   Like an over-enthusiastic gobshite fae Bellshill.

Jo   Who's just looked up all the words for great in the thesaurus.

Sammy (*as* **Ally**)   Make no mistake about it, the brilliant Scotland team today face maybe their toughest opponents yet – the incredible Chileans who are very . . . (*checks thesaurus*) fabulous. After fantastic wins over the inspiring Spain and outstanding Italy.

But let me say, this is set up for a tight game. It really is. We aren't expecting a huge amount of goals for either team. Whoever wins it'll likely be a one or maximum two goal margin. This may well be the closest match of the tournament so far. Too tight to call . . .

A shift.

Jo   Noor! Noor! Head up. Fucking pass.

All (*except* **Jo**)   YAAAASSSSSS!

A shift.

Sammy (*as* **Ally**)   Final score Scotland 5, Chile 0. Unbelievable! With their star player Noor showing she's head and shoulders above the rest on the park with a hat trick. What a talent! Absolutely brilliant. The Scottish wonder kid.

A chant is taught to the audience.

Ooh. Ah. Up The Noor.

Said. Ooh. Ah. Up The Noor.

The B   Clever that like. Changing the words to 'Up The Noor' because at the Celtic games we sing Up The RA.

Lorraine   The RA?

The B   The IRA, Lorraine.

Lorraine   I didn't know you were Catholic?

The B   Abso-fucking-lutely. Have you seen my tattoo?

The B *shows the rest of the team her back tattoo.*

Lorraine   Is that the Pope?

The B   Aye, wearing a Celtic top.

Lorraine   That's really something, B.

Noor *enters.*

Noor   Finals here we comeeeee.

Lorraine   Noor, you're our Hat-trick hero!

Noor   Says you ya Clean Sheet Cat.

Sammy   Noor, when you did those step overs before your first goal I actually let out a little wee, I couldn't help myself. That's the most excited I've been since Paul was born.

The B   And that Crufts turn you did right before the second goal. Totally amazing.

Noor   You mean Cruyff turn but I'll take it.

The B   I thought it was a Crufts turn, like with the dogs round the cones and that?

Noor   Never mind.

Lorraine   Oh! Oh! But what about Noor's third goal? Chipping it over the player like she was playing golf or something. Then a half volley into the Top Bins!

The B   Check you Lorraine man with the terminology – chipping it and half volleys and Top Bins man. C'mon the Cat!

Sammy   You're a bit quiet, Jo?

Jo   It's nothing.

Sammy   I thought you'd be buzzing. 5 – 0. Into the final eh? What's up?

Jo   I said it's nothing.

Sammy   Alright.

Noor   Guys, I hate to be that lassie but maybe you could sign my match ball?

All apart from **Jo**   Aye of course! Sure thing, etc.

Noor   Thanks. I'm going to give it to Nana for his birthday.

Lorraine   He'll be so proud of you, darling. Top scorer.

The B   I'm not usually into lads, but see if we win this tournament I'll be straight up to the commentary box to see if Baggio will Italia my 90 if you catch my drift?

Lorraine   Sorry?

The B   Paolo my Maldini, if you see what I mean.

Lorraine   Eh?

The B   Inter my Milan if you see where I'm going?

Lorraine   You've completely lost me.

Noor   Do you want to sign it, Jo?

Jo   You should have passed.

The B   What you fucking say?

Jo   She should have fucking passed. It's not high school.

Sammy   She made it look like school though. We all did. By working as a tea –

Jo   Nah. It was embarrassing. We're here to win.

Lorraine   We did win, Jo!

Jo   We looked like wee lassies out there.

Noor   What you talking about?

Jo   You didn't fucking pass to me.

Noor   I passed to you loads.

Jo   You know what I'm talking about.

Sammy   Jo, maybe we should go outside for a bit of fresh air, eh? Let's not ruin a good afternoon.

Jo   A good afternoon? For who?

The B   Hiy we got to the final, man, what's all this huffing and puffing.

Lorraine   Yeah, you need to Chile out, Jo!

The B   Don't think this is the time, mate.

Lorraine   Sorry.

Noor   I know what this is. You think when I chipped it over that blonde lassie I should've passed to you, is that it?

Jo   You've been doing this the whole tournament. Selfish choices, every game. I'm free in space but you always do whatever is going to make you look better.

Noor   But you said to put myself first . . .

Jo   Three goals. It's greedy, Noor.

The B   She needs to calm the fuck down, or I'll lose it like.

Jo   Go on then. Lose it.

Noor   I was trying to win. For us. For you.

Jo   Save it. You want to be the best. But you're just a wee lassie. You haven't been through what I've been through. To be here. I've had to fight. You're not a team player.

The B   Jo, this is out of order like.

Noor I'm not a team player? I've scored half our goals in this tournament. Got like a hunner assists. And you're telling me I'm not a team player?

Jo I'm here to win the World Cup. And you're letting me down.

The B You're letting us down, Jo. The so-called Captain. Depressing us rather than lifting us up. Moaning at us rather than inspiring us. And picking on the youngest player in the team that's just scored a fucking hat trick to get us into the final? Get tae fuck.

Jo I am the Captain. You're not listening to me –

The B I SAID GET TAE FUCK BEFORE I –

Noor B, calm down.

Sammy Jo, let's go, come on.

Jo Stuff your fucking match ball.

Sammy *and* **Jo** *exit.*

The B FUCK MAN. Should've kicked that fucking cunt's heid in.

Noor B, take a breath, eh? Sit down.

Lorraine That's a bit far, Bethany . . .

The B Back to Bethany are we, Lorraine? Knew it was a fucking act. Away and clean the fucking grass or something fucking Keira Shiteley. Fucking bend it up your hoop ya fucking fud. Fuck sake.

Lorraine I think we should all just take a moment. I'm going to go and get a cup of tea.

Lorraine *leaves.*

The B Aye away you fuck. Cunts. Lot of them.

Noor Just breathe, B.

The B Us two need to stick together like.

SASHA

Jo   I run.

Fucking sprint.

Bunch of backstabbing bastards. Just like that mad painting.

I pelt it.

Past the pitches.
Past bars.
Past ice creams.
Past pints.
Past happy fucking families.

I stop.

I'm standing in a big, massive church.

It's fucking huge.

The windows make this multi-coloured glow that fills the room.

Paintings.

Statues.

Columns.

Gold.

Marble.

Expensive.

How many millions are in this room?

Fuck me.

Space.

So much space.

Useless space.

Imagine all the problems that could be solved if you sold everything in here.

How many folk could get a sleep in here rather than being out in the pishing rain?

Jesus is like a dragon. Sitting on a big pile of money that we don't have. That we need.

My last foster family were religious, right? Took me to church. To mass. Got me confirmed. But when I needed them. They said I was too much.

How's that community?

When I couldnae get clean, they cared more about going to church than me.

When I went to rehab for the first time.

They prayed.

What fucking use is praying?

Football's my religion. I've been playing since Primary 5 and that's when I realised it was my calling. When I step onto the pitch nothing else matters.

See the thing about my story is . . . It's my story. I choose when I tell it. And when I don't. These lassies think they know everything about me. You think you know everything about me. But you dinnae.

There is one person I can count on. Sasha. We were on the same team together. She was on the wing – same position Noor plays. Me up front. Amazing combination, a wee dream team. She'd cross it over and I'd knock it in the back of the net. The creator and the finisher. Brilliant, man.

I leave the church and go to a wee pub I find at the end of the road.

I stand outside.

Hands are shaking.

Haven't touched anything in fourteen month.

But I hurt.

This hurts.

See when I started using, Sasha withdrew from me. Didn't like it, ken? Why would she? She could see what it was doing to me.

It didn't stop her trying it though. Aye. She hated it, obviously. Everyone hates their first time.

And it killed her. The worst thing that could've happened. I'll be honest, I wanted to die too. Sometimes I still do. Should've been me like. But it wasnae.

So whenever I feel like this. Low enough to go back to using. I take a breath and speak to Sasha. Just a wee one-way conversation with her so that I can remind myself why I'm here. For her. For me.

When we were younger, you always said that we'd play for Scotland. Win the World Cup together. Look. I'm here.

But the green glow of the pub is so inviting.

COACH SPEECH

Sammy (*as* **Coach**)   Gather round, ladies. I said gather round.

Noor (*as* **Coach**)   I hear there's been some disagreements. To say the least. Look . . .

The B (*as* **Coach**)   Look, I've got a confession.

Sammy (*as* **Coach**)   I know I've not been the best Coach for us.

Lorraine (*as* **Coach**)   For you.

The B (*as* **Coach**)   Coming and going with the divorce and that. I should've left it off the pitch but it's been hard.

Sammy (*as* **Coach**)   In our first session together I laid out six values. Six ways of how we were going to be a team.

Lorraine (*as* **Coach**)   And regrettably, every one of those six values has been undermined. By all of us, myself included. Broken. But not irreparably.

Noor (*as* **Coach**)   We've come so far, *so far.* I'm so immensely proud of every single one of you.

The B (*as* **Coach**)   Each one of you has made a difference here. Without every one of you we wouldn't be here. In the final. The fucking final, ladies.

Sammy (*as* **Coach**)   So, let's not give this up now.

Jo   Players always come first.

The B   I cannae fucking hear yous . . .

Jo   Players always come first.

All   Aye.

Jo   We look to the future.

All   Aye.

Jo   We never leave anyone behind.

All   AYE.

Jo   We place others before self.

All   AYE.

Jo   We keep our promises.

All   AYE!

Jo   And we are a family.

All   AYE!

Jo   Same team?

All   SAME TEAM.

THE FINAL

The B (*as* **Baggio**)   We're here! It's the final of the Homeless World Cup. Scotland vs Bosnia & Herzegovina, it's a liiiiveee.

Sammy (*as* **Ally**)   What a journey it's been for both teams. The brilliant high-scoring Scotland on one hand.

Lorraine (*as* **Souness**)   And the ultra-defensive Bosnia on the other.

The B (*as* **Baggio**)   Niente Scozia, niente festa.

Sammy (*as* **Ally**)   What does that mean, Roberto?

The B (*as* **Baggio**)   No Scotland, no party!

Lorraine/Souness   I think Scotland should count themselves lucky to be here actually.

Sammy (*as* **Ally**)   I disagree, Graeme, I have to say. Scotland have been unbelievable at this tournament. I can't wait to see them out on the park tonight for what should be an absolutely brilliant final.

The B (*as* **Baggio**)   Here we go then, the final of the Homeless Women's World Cup.

And itssssaaaaliiiiiiiiiiiiiveeee.

The team sing the national anthem. The audience – Scots or not – are encouraged to sing along.

The B *performs her ritual one last time.*

Jo (*to audience*)   I pull my captain's armband on. And I'm proud y'know? Proud to be playing for Scotland. For you. For us.

I shake the hand of the other captain. They're sweaty. She's nervous. I'm no.

Tails.

We'll go into the sun first half and make it easier in the second.

I wave Noor over.

She's all sheepish like she thinks she's in bother.

I look at her. I think about Sasha. I always think about Sasha when I look at her.

I wish you were here. Playing right next to me.

Jo *hugs* **Noor**.

Let's go fucking win this, pal.

(*To audience*.) And we're off.

The B (*to audience*) Who would have thought Bethany McGuigan at the World Cup final?

Sammy (*to audience*) As soon as the whistle goes the Bosnians hoof a long ball up the field.

Jo (*to audience*) Getting stuck right in about us.

The B (*to audience*) They think they can tackle, eh? I'll show them a tackle.

Noor (*to audience*) The Bosnian striker looks a bit like a female David Beckham back when he had the frosted tips.

Lorraine (*to audience*) She tries to shoot from miles out.

Noor (*to audience*) It's a pure peach.

The B (*to audience*) But I dive in the way and block it with my arse.

Sammy Let's be having ye!

The B (*to audience*) I nod back at Lorraine to say: 'I've got this.'

Lorraine (*to audience*) I pass up to Sammy who touches it inside.

Sammy (*to audience*)   And what a touch, man.

Jo (*to audience*)   Noor takes it up the wing and –

The B   HIY. WATCH WHAT YOU'RE FUCKING DOING.

Lorraine (*to audience*)   One of their defenders, who looks like a female Vinnie Jones with a bob, has gone into the back of wee Noor.

The B   YOU'RE A FUCKING DISGRACE. AND YOU PLAY SHITE FOOTBALL.

Sammy (*to audience*)   The ref gives her a look.

Jo   Calm down, B.

Lorraine   Float like a butterfly, sting like a bee.

Noor   Just breathe, B.

Sammy   You've come this far.

Noor   Just breathe.

The B (*to audience*)   But all I can see is red.

Noor (*to audience*)   Sprint to every ball.

Sammy (*to audience*)   Press at every opportunity.

Jo (*to audience*)   Keep the pressure on.

The B (*to audience*)   This is the final.

Jo (*to audience*)   One touch.

Lorraine (*to audience*)   Pass.

Sammy (*to audience*)   Go.

The B (*to audience*)   One touch.

Noor (*to audience*)   Pass.

All (*to audience*)   Go.

Jo (*to audience*)   Tackle.

The B   Fuck!

Lorraine (*to audience*)   Bosnian Becks shoots . . .

Sammy (*to audience*)   But the Cat is there to save it.

The B (*to audience*)   Course she is.

Noor (*to audience*)   She rolls it out to Jo, who passes the ball to me and I –

All   Oooft.

Jo (*to audience*)   Vinnie Jones goes right into the back of Noor.

The B (*to audience*)   Again.

Lorraine (*to audience*)   Her legs snap together like a pair of scissors.

Sammy (*to audience*)   She hits the deck.

Noor   Refe-fucking-ree.

Jo (*to audience*)   And there's a roar.

Noor (*to audience*)   But it's no me.

Sammy (*to audience*)   And it's not Vinnie.

Lorraine (*to audience*)   It's The B.

Jo (*to audience*)   And you can see why they call her The B.

Lorraine (*to audience*)   Not Bethany.

Sammy (*to audience*)   The B.

Noor (*to audience*)   The one and only.

Lorraine (*to audience*)   Because she's charging across the pitch like a grizzly bear.

Sammy (*to audience*)   She scoops the lassie onto her feet and takes a step back.

Jo (*to audience*)   And just like Zinedine Zidane.

Noor (*to audience*)   Sticks the nut in her.

Sammy (*to audience*)   Bone to bone.

Jo (*to audience*)   Skull to skull.

Lorraine (*to audience*)   Cranium to cranium.

The B   You leave my wee pal alone.

Sammy (*to audience*)   And now, she's getting dragged off the pitch.

Jo (*to audience*)   Our best defender.

Lorraine (*to audience*)   Straight red and sent to the changing rooms.

The B   Fuck.

Jo (*to audience*)   Down to four at the turn of the half and they've got a free kick.

Sammy (*to audience*)   No one ever scores these things.

Noor (*to audience*)   Becks steps up.

Jo (*to audience*)   The English David Beckham used to bang the free kicks in, man.

Noor (*to audience*)   But looking like someone doesnae mean you possess the same skills as them.

Jo   You're right.

Lorraine (*to audience*)   She gets her head down.

Sammy (*to audience*)   Bosnian Beckham takes a run-up.

Noor (*to audience*)   And . . .

Lorraine (*to audience*)   Goal.

Jo (*to audience*)   This wasn't supposed to happen. Not like this.

Sammy (*to audience*)   Half time.

Noor (*to audience*)   Bosnia 1. Scotland 0.

The dressing room. **The B**. *Is staring into space. Emotionless, broken, almost traumatised.*

Noor   What the fuck just happened?

Sammy   I feel like I've been put through the washing machine.

Lorraine   B. B. Are you ok?

The B *doesn't respond.*

Jo   I've never seen her like this.

Lorraine   Is there anything we can get you?

Jo   B?

Lorraine   You don't have to speak if you don't want to. Just know that we're here.

Noor   Nadeem hasn't text me. He was supposed to text me when Nana was watching the stream. He's useless.

Sammy   FUCKING LITTLE PRICK.

Jo   Are you alright?

Sammy   NO I'M NOT ALRIGHT!

Lorraine   What's wrong hen?

Sammy   A PARTY? A FUCKING PARTY? I'LL KILL HIM. MURDER HIM.

Jo   We've got a match to finish.

Noor   Nana said he'd be watching. Do you think everything's alright?

Sammy   I GO AWAY FOR ONE FUCKING WEEK. THAT UNGRATEFUL LITTLE BASTARD.

Jo   C'mon let's focus.

Noor   His phone's dead.

Lorraine   B? Are you ok?

The B   I've done it again.

Everyone looks at **The B** *now that she's finally spoken.*

The B   When I was inside the counsellor said I had too much emotions, right? That I struggled to channel them. And it was all to do with the people I care about.

Noor   So it's like an honour you headbutted someone for me?

The B   Nah. I shouldnae have done it. But kind of aye.

Noor   It's nice to be looked after for once.

Lorraine   You're my man of the match.

Sammy   Woman of the match.

Noor   Heidbutt of the match.

Lorraine (*to audience*)   I heard The B always stands up for her friends.

Sammy (*to audience*)   I heard The B taught me how to believe in myself.

Noor (*to audience*)   I heard The B is the only reason I'm here.

The B   Cheers, eh? I've never been this close to a group of lassies before. Folk are always more interested in the rumours about me than actual me.

Nobody knows I did what I did cause my dah was a beast.

Got done for manslaughter.

You can hurt me all you want but nobody touches my wee brother and sister. My family. Simple as that.

Everyone hugs **The B**.

The B   Finish the job.

Jo We will.

Sammy We've still got one more half to play.

Lorraine Let's leave it all on the field ladies.

Noor For B.

The B For us.

Jo Same team?

All Same team.

A shift.

Sammy (*to audience*) I'm on the pitch.

Lorraine (*to audience*) She's flying.

Noor (*to audience*) Flying from challenge to challenge.

Sammy (*to audience*) Every ball is mine.

Noor (*to audience*) We're raging.

Sammy (*to audience*) Raging about Daryll.

Jo (*to audience*) Raging about losing.

Lorraine (*to audience*) Raging about The B.

Sammy (*to audience*) I stick my foot in as hard as I can to tackle their striker.

Noor (*to audience*) A big biting tackle just like B taught us in training.

Jo (*to audience*) Sammy picks up the ball and does a wee dribble

Sammy (*to audience*) Without thinking I do a step over – a fucking step over – you'll be mad you're missing this, Daryll!

Lorraine (*to audience*) Her heart is pumping but she's in total control.

Sammy (*to audience*) I pass to Jo who feeds Noor . . .

Jo (*to audience*)   Noor takes a touch and –

All   YASSSSSSSSS. CMONNNNNNNNN.

Sammy (*to audience*)   Equaliser.

Jo (*to audience*)   Game on.

Noor (*to audience*)   I wish Nana had seen that.

Lorraine (*to audience*)   But that's fired the Bosnians right up.

Noor (*to audience*)   Sammy makes another brilliant challenge to stop a Bosnian attack and passes to Jo.

Jo (*to audience*)   But Vinnie Jones crashes into me.

Sammy (*to audience*)   Jo's taken one for the team there . . .

Noor (*to audience*)   The ball bounces to me, I see a gap, a small sight of goal, and this is it, I swing my leg back and . . .

All (*to audience*)   CRUNCH.

Jo (*to audience*)   Penalty.

Noor (*to audience*)   Finally!

Sammy   Get it up ye!

Lorraine (*to audience*)   And the crowd goes wild.

Jo (*to the audience*)   Go wild then!

The crowd goes wild.

Jo (*to the audience*)   I said go fucking wild then!

The crowd goes even wilder.

Noor (*to audience*)   Right at the death.

Jo (*to audience*)   I turn to see Noor picking up the ball and . . . handing it to me.

Noor   You take it.

Jo   I cannae.

Noor   How?

Jo   We agreed that you're on pens. You're the best at them. You've been the best all tournament.

Noor   You're our Captain. And I would've given up if it wasn't for you.

Jo   You wouldn't have.

Noor   Aye I would have. When you're my age folk ask you all the time what you want to be when you grow up. I want to be like you.

Jo   You don't want to be like me.

Noor   I do. One day you'll be running this hing. And I'll be the captain. So I've got plenty of time to take penalties in the future.

Jo   You calling me old?

Noor   Just take it.

Jo   Are you sure?

Noor   You deserve this.

Jo (*to audience*)   So I take the ball. I place it on the spot. I breathe and I look up to Sasha. I plant my foot flat on the ground. Bend my knee as I bring my kicking foot down, keeping my planted foot steady. Using not just my legs but my whole body. Leaning right over the ball, just like Noor said. Everything has been leading to this. I breathe. And I strike.

Sammy (*to audience*)   And the baw takes flight.

The B (*to audience*)   Soars like a fucking meteor.

Noor (*to audience*)   She's smashed it.

The B (*to audience*)   Hard as fuck.

Sammy (*to audience*)   Fae her legs.

Lorraine (*to audience*)   Comes pure power.

The B (*to audience*)   Flames coming oot the back of the ball.

Sammy (*to audience*)   This time there actually was.

Lorraine (*to audience*)   And it rockets.

Noor (*to audience*)   Thunders.

Sammy (*to audience*)   Hurtles.

The B (*to audience*)   Towards the . . .

Lorraine (*to audience*)   The ball ricochets off the bar.

Jo *sinks to the floor, her head in her hands.*

Lorraine (*to audience*)   The Bosnians turn and they are all running at us like a tidal wave.

There's too many of them. The girls are all looking at me. Their Cat. Their only hope. Bosnian Beckham strikes so I stick my leg out to stop the shot, thinking not today, not this time.

But the ball crashes through my legs . . . and into the back of the net.

Bosnia 2. Scotland 1.

The final whistle goes. It's over. We've lost.

THE AFTERMATH

Jo   You were the designated penalty taker. I should've made you take it.

Noor   It's my fault. I asked you. I didn't . . .

Jo   Didn't think I was going to miss? Neither did I.

Noor   It doesn't matter now.

Lorraine   A nutmeg. A fucking nutmeg.

The B   Oi, careful with your language, Lorraine hen. Better wash your fucking mouth out. And since when did you add nutmeg to your footballing vocabulary?

Sammy   You're a bit chirpy, B.

Lorraine   You do know we lost, right?

The B   Aye course. I was out in the stands, fucking gutted. But seeing yous all out there, playing your fucking hearts out like Sarina's Lionesses mixed with Barca 09 with a wee bit of Stevie Clarke's Tartan Army sprinkled on top. It was fucking magic man. Come on get back out there!

Noor   What?

The B   Everyone's waiting on you. They're gonnae dae you a guard of honour.

Noor   Whit's a guard of honour?

The B   The wee clappy tunnel thing.

Jo   We lost.

The B   It's just a game of fitba.

Jo   But . . . it still hurts.

Noor   We came all this way.

The B   Aye. And you're all fucking superstars.

Jo   I missed.

Sammy   I should have made that tackle.

Lorraine   She put it through my legs.

Noor   I just stood and watched.

The B   Yous killed it. Even Bosnian Vinnie Jones said so.

Sammy   Who?

The B   Vinnie, the lassie a nutted. I said I was sorry, and so did she for crunching ye's aw. She said she's got a problem wae the red mist tae. We've a lot in common actually. Proper sound cunt. Bastard on the pitch but, my kind of lady. So, let's get back out there.

Jo   I think we're good here.

The B   Come and see the fans.

Sammy   B?! Leave it, eh?

The B   Nah. Yous wouldnae leave me when I needed picking back up. You of all people Sammy. Cannae expect folk to leave you when you wouldnae leave them. You were on fire out there.

Sammy   Nah I wasnae. Same old me, crap as ever.

Noor   Nah. You were class.

Lorraine   You were, Sammy.

Noor   You were like the Hulk. No the Change Centre one. The actual one.

The B   Raging and charging around the pitch. Filling my boots.

Sammy   I don't know about that.

The B   You always wondered why you were here. But you're the glue, eh? Sticking us all together. And wee Noor, we couldnae have got here without you. You're no gonnae forget about us when you're famous, are you?

Noor   Don't know about that like.

The B   And Lorraine. You did my pan in since day dot. And I didnae really ever think I'd be friends with someone like you.

Lorraine   Someone like me?

The B   Aye – eh –

Lorraine   Only joking.

The B   Ya cheeky cow!

Lorraine   I've learnt so much from you. I thought I needed a guidebook but all I needed to do was follow your lead.

The B   That's cheesy as fuck, Lorraine . . . but I appreciate it.

Noor   Why are you being like nice and that?

The B   If yous tell anyone what I'm fucking saying I'll do the same thing to yous that I did to my dah. Only joking. But seriously, we will be remembered for what we did here. People will remember us for playing the best football, in the best team.

And Jo. We would've all patched it if it wasn't for you. You've pretty much been our Coach the whole time.

Jo   I need to get something off my chest. I'm just going to say it. I was at a pub before the game.

Noor   Shit.

Lorraine   Are you alright?

Jo   Aye fine, aye. It's not what you think. I was gutted at how I behaved. After the Chile game my head was a mess. So I went there. I was outside just staring at it for what felt like an hour. And there was only one thing that stopped me going in.

Lorraine   We had a game to play.

Jo   No. Aye. We did. But not that. I knew that what is here in this room, when I'm with yous, that feeling, what you girls give me as part of this team is stronger and more powerful than anything a drink could ever give me. In here, I'm surrounded by my sisters, a family. Fuck the final. Fuck the fucking football. Same team.

All   Same team!

Coach *enters.*

Jo (*as* **Coach**)   Alright ladies. Did I miss something?

Noor   Are you kidding me?

Jo (*as* **Coach**)   Sorry about that. I would've come to deliver an inspiring, uplifting speech about what you all mean to me and how it was never about the football but I knew one of you would've had it covered. My phone's been buzzing off the hook since the final whistle. The Mrs called and I can move back in. Aw and Sammy, I'm just off the phone with Daryll.

Sammy   No don't . . .

Jo (*as* **Coach**)   Well actually it wasn't just Daryll. Paul was there too. And their grandmother.

Sammy   My maw was there?

Jo (*as* **Coach**)   Aye and Noor's Nana and Nadeem anaw.

Noor   At Daryll's party?

Sammy   They were watching the game?

Jo (*as* **Coach**)   Why do you think they were all together?

Noor   So Nana saw my goal?

Jo (*as* **Coach**)   Of course. They all started singing 'Yes Sir, I Can Boogie' at the end of the match. They're still singing it now.

Noor   Class. Even though we didn't win?

Lorraine   We did win. In all the ways that matter anyway.

The B   My Cat.

Lorraine   'Yes Sir, I Can Boogie.' Is that not the song you were singing in the changing room showers yesterday?

The B   Hiy, I swore you to secrecy over that.

Noor   That's a tune!

Lorraine   I think it's about time we had a boogie . . .

Sammy   And you do owe us after that Zinedine Zidane headbutt . . .

Noor   Binedine Bidane!

The B   Very good.

Jo   Go on B.

The B   Well . . . you know I've always wanted to be a singer like . . .

The B *sings 'Yes Sir, I Can Boogie'.*

The audience join in with the chorus. It is celebratory, triumphant, euphoric.

This segways into 'No Scotland, No Party' which the audience can still be singing as they leave the theatre space.

The End.

Printed in the USA
CPSIA information can be obtained
at www.ICGtesting.com
LVHW020853171024
794056LV00002B/515